D1598395

RETHINKING
CLINICAL
TECHNIQUE

RETHINKING CLINICAL TECHNIQUE

FRED BUSCH, Ph.D.

JASON ARONSON INC.
Northvale, New Jersey
London

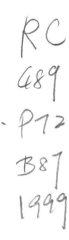

This book was set in 12 pt. Galliard.

Library of Congress Cataloging-in-Publication Data

Busch, Fred, 1939–
    Rethinking clinical technique / Fred Busch.
        p. cm.
    Includes bibliographical references and index.
    ISBN 0-7657-0183-9 (hardcover : alk. paper)
    1. Psychodynamic psychotherapy. 2. Ego (Psychology) 3. Object relations (Psychoanalysis) 4. Psychoanalysis. I. Title.
    RC489.P72B87   1999
    616.89'14—dc21   98–30372

Printed in the United States of America on acid-free paper. For information and catalog write to Jason Aronson Inc., 230 Livingston Street, Northvale, New Jersey 07647-1726. Or visit our website: http://www.aronson.com

To Paul Gray and Marvin Margolis

In his own way each has changed the nature of the debates within psychoanalysis.

Griefs, at the moment they change into ideas, lose some of their power to injure our heart.

—Marcel Proust

Contents

1

Some Current Myths in Psychoanalytic Technique

Two theses inform this monograph. The first is that we have developed and nurtured certain myths in conceptualizing the psychoanalytic method, and these have come to dominate our thinking about clinical technique and the goals of analysis. The result has been a developmental lag (Gray 1982) in certain areas of technique, while other areas have hypertrophied. Techniques considered basic to psychoanalysis have never been fully explicated, and misunderstanding of the potential usefulness of these techniques flourishes. A prime example of this is resistance analysis (Busch 1992, 1995a, Gray 1982, 1994), which has been championed by some and skewered by others. From another perspective, insights into human behavior and technical considerations gleaned from those working within clinical models considered outside the purview of traditional psychoanalysis have been seen as offering a challenge to clinical technique, rather than as adding additional information to our fund of knowledge. The ongoing antipathy between what has become known as the classical analysts and the relational school, the self psychologists, interpersonalists, intersubjectivists, and object relationalists is an example of what Richards (1995) calls the "policy of exclusion," which has dominated our political and clinical thinking. By identifying the myths that feed some of these conflicts of theory and technique, I hope to clear a path toward those areas where there may be common ground.

My second thesis is that we are in danger of losing some essential ingredient of what Levy calls Freud's radical treatment (personal communication, 1996). This ingredient, which

I would characterize as greater psychological well-being via understanding one's own mind, is immeasurably bolstered using new insights into the theory and technique of clinical psychoanalysis from the realm of ego psychology. By understanding the central role of the ego in the change process in psychoanalysis, new methods of conceptualizing the clinical task of understanding and interpreting become available to us. These new methods, some of which are old methods rediscovered and put in previously unspecified clinical contexts, are designed to identify, analyze, or capitalize on those factors that work against and for structural changes in the ego. These changes are basic to what I would consider a psychoanalytic treatment, in contrast to a therapeutic one. An alteration in how the mind works is our fundamental connection to Freud's psychoanalysis, and it is in danger of being lost in the increasing emphasis on the ameliorative effects of the relationship.

Although I agree with many of the critiques brought against the way psychoanalysis has been practiced by those more attuned to the significance of the analytic relationship, it is the omission of a coherent theory of mind and how psychoanalysis can bring about significant changes in analysands' views of their own thought processes that differentiates our perspectives. I hope to demonstrate that structural change in the ego is fundamental to the psychoanalytic process, and that we need to be aware of methods of working that aid or hinder this process. Let me begin with the myths.

Myth #1

Myth #1 is that American psychoanalysis has been dominated by ego psychology. Wallerstein's (1988) view of "ego psychology," universally accepted since the '50s, as holding a monolithic hegemony over the psychoanalytic domain in America, must be examined closely. I believe it has been one of our most enduring and complex myths, dominating the thinking of critics and defenders of so-called classical analysis.

It is my impression that is primarily in three areas that ego psychology has dominated thinking in American psychoanalysis over the last half century. The first of these is the area of the developing ego in its environmental surrounds, and the investigation of conditions leading to either a flourishing of or interference with ego functioning. Foreshadowed in the work of Anna Freud (1936) and Hartmann (1939), its first convincing demonstration was in Spitz's (1945, 1946) work on "hospitalism," which showed the devastating effects of maternal deprivation, followed by Erikson's (1950) interpretation of the threatening or affirmative feelings associated with the nature of the resolution of the psychosexual stages. Mahler's (Mahler et al. 1975) work on the separation-individuation subphases is an example of how ego psychology was developed and utilized in the United States in a manner unlike that used anywhere else in the world. By pointing to the developmental sequence of certain anxieties, and the disruptive consequences for the child of the unavailability (emotional or physical) of needed objects, Mahler pointed clinicians to a greater understanding of one of the factors in the ego's capacity to tolerate anxiety in the face of a threatened loss (either real or imagined). It has become another possible explanatory cause in the analyst's understanding of threats to the ego, and finds immediate currency in the work of Pine (1985), who helps us understand how such problems might manifest themselves in the analytic situation, for example, in distinguishing between separation problems where there is "differentiated other" (p. 233) and those where there has been a "failure of differentiation" (p. 233). In short, the mapping of the effect of environmental and developmental factors on ego functioning has had extraordinary impact on our thinking about human development, and can be seen in the marked changes in our views about childhood and adolescence, and such diverse clinical concepts as action, narcissism, and trauma, just to name a few.

The second important contribution of American ego psychology appears in the 1938–1959 work of Rapaport (Rapaport 1967) and involved the increasingly sophisticated diagnosis of psychological states based on the intactness of the ego. It led to significant changes in how we understood pathology, and shifted diagnostic understanding from its primary emphasis on dynamics to diagnosis, which investigated the intactness of the patient's ego in all its manifestations. It is demonstrated at its most succinct in Zetzel's (1968) classic paper, "The So-Called Good Hysteric," and at its most exhaustive in Kernberg's (1976) delineation of the syndrome of the borderline personality organization. It has led to sweeping changes in what type of patients we believe can be treated in psychoanalysis, and the development of special methods of interpretation in dealing with more disturbed patients.

The third major contribution of American ego psychology was Brenner's (1982) conceptualization of mental content as a compromise formation, which crystallized the significance of contributions from the agencies of the mind on any mental act. This led us to understand, for example, that in the psychoanalytic setting any content can be used as a resistance, and that dreams are more than just the experience of a drive derivative. Thus the concept of compromise formation has allowed for the possibility of a more richly textured view of the ego. A patient's increasingly hostile behavior toward the analyst can be seen not only as an expression of a sadistic impulse, but also as response of the unconscious ego to any one of myriad of threatening thoughts and feelings. Unconscious fantasies, seen primarily as an expression of a drive derivative, could also be looked at from the side of the resistances, while their effects on ego functions could also be explored (Arlow 1969). Paradoxically, Brenner's views on compromise formation have led him to de-emphasize the significance of highlighting the ego in clinical technique with, as we shall see, important consequences.

What we have not had is an agree-upon clinical model that utilizes even the rudimentary principles of ego psychology. Let us briefly look at the most basic of ego psychological principles underlying technique, that which was fundamental in causing Freud to switch from the topographic to the structural model: unconscious resistances. Gray (1982) and I (Busch 1992) have documented the significant differences among analysts in the application of resistance analysis. While the credo of defense analysis before content analysis was trumpeted by American psychoanalysts, examination of the specifics led to the realization of widely held differences, most often based on the degree to which analysts followed Freud's (1926) second theory of anxiety. However, in our literature we have tended to idealize our understanding of resistance analysis, and perpetuated a myth of an unbroken theoretical line from Freud's conversion to the structural model to Anna Freud to present-day analysts (see Pray [1994] on the difference in resistance analysis between Anna Freud and Brenner). As we shall see, it is one of many myths perpetrated about the solidity and uniformity of our ego psychological heritage in clinical practice.

Myth #2

Myth #2 is that we already have a well-articulated clinical model that takes into account the role of the ego, and this can be found in the work of the primary translators of the structural model over the past thirty years, Arlow and Brenner. When Brenner (1994) tells us it is time to discard the structural model, and jettisons the concept of an ego, does this represent a major shift in thinking from one of those most identified with the structural model and the clinical consideration of the ego? It will be my argument that Brenner's recent statement on the topic is not a major shift in his thinking. Rather he has now made explicit what has been implicit in his and others' thinking on ego psychology in relationship to clinical technique. In broad brush strokes my position is that Arlow and Brenner's interpretation of the structural model with regard to psychoanalytic technique does not utilize the concepts of an ego psychological approach as I understand it. Their underlying model is a departure from the ego psychology of the 1950s and '60s. The concept of compromise formation, so useful in understanding psychoanalytic data, may not always be so useful as a cornerstone of psychoanalytic technique.

Myth #3

Myth #3 is that working at the surface is akin to working superficially with the clinical material. Analysts working within an ego psychological perspective have described the importance of working at the surface (Davison et al. 1990, Levy and Inderbitzen 1990, Paniagua 1985, 1991). Levy and Inderbitzen's (1990) concept of the analytic surface and Paniagua's (1991) distinction between the patient surface, the analyst's surface, and the workable surface are attempts to define what in the analysand's material can be most fruitfully paid attention to so that important material can be explored in an emotionally meaningful manner for the patient. Yet, I am impressed with how many clinicians still equate the depth of an interpretation with its profundity. Anna Freud's (1965) description of the early antipathy between work on the surface and the depth remains a current cautionary tale.

> In the earliest era of psychoanalytic work . . . there was a marked tendency to keep the relations between analysis and surface observations wholly negative and hostile. This was the time of the discovery of the unconscious mind and of the gradual evolvement of the analytic method, two directions of work which were inextricably bound up with each other. It was then the task of the analytic pioneers to stress the dif-

ference between observable and hidden impulses rather than the similarities between them and, more important than that, to establish the fact in the first instance that there existed such hidden, i.e., unconscious motivation. [p. 32]

It is my impression that we still struggle with how to work with the analytic surface in a way that leads to deeper understanding and is emotionally meaningful to the patient. We too often confuse our sense that we are empathically attuned with the patient's unconscious with the patient's ability to constructively use this information.

Myth #4

Myth #4 is that ego psychology is an instinctual-based theory that is mechanistic in its approach. Schools of thought that emphasize the primacy of object relations have typically linked ego psychology with drive theory (e.g., "American drive-defense ego psychological analysts" [Spezzano 1993, p. 224]). I would agree that for many years the structural model remained far more tied to an instinctual base than was acknowledged, while we maintained a highly ambivalent view of past and current object relations in our clinical theory. This occurred even though Freud's study of the role of narcissism and object relationships predated the structural model (Freud 1914, 1917).

Yet, forays into other explanatory constructs as determinants of behavior by those embracing the structural model have tended to be ignored by analysts presenting ego psychology as drive dominated. Contemporary ego psychology considers drive derivatives as one factor in the formation of symptoms and their alleviation. In fact, there is little in contemporary psychoanalytic theories that is alien to an ego psychological perspective.

The analyst's affective involvement, as both a necessary and inevitable component of any successful analysis (Renik 1993), has not been sufficiently acknowledged in the literature on ego psychology. The analyst's absorption of painful affects in the service of approaching the ego in an experience-near manner is the everyday fare of defense analysis. However, it has not been adequately recognized by critics of ego psychology that one of the primary factors in Freud's move toward the structural theory was the discovery of unconscious affects as a prime determinant of behavior (Freud 1926). Effective resistance analysis, for example, is all about affects. Mitchell's (1988) depiction of resistance analysis in classical theory, which is consistent among the schools of object relations, does not take into account the developments in Freud's theory after 1914.

> The analyst, whose function is to investigate and uncover, is pitted against the resistances, whose function is to protect and keep hidden the infantile wishes and longings. The ultimate aim of psychoanalysis is to overcome the resistance, to flush out the beast to "track down the libido . . . withdrawn into its hiding place" (Freud 1912), to tame the infantile wishes by uncovering them through memory. [p. 281]

Jacobson (1993) has borrowed a Mafia term to comment on this particular method of sinking what became known as "drive-defense theory," labeling it the "cement-overshoes technique" (p. 539). He goes on to state that if one presents structural theory as an "abstract, unempathic, mechanistic model which forces a patient's every utterance into an oedipal mold, and which demands a rigid, stereotyped blank screen technique, then of course one can understand a wish to leave it behind" (p. 539). Mitchell's (Mitchell and Black 1995) recent work presents a greater appreciation for the importance of affect regulation in ego psychology, and resistance analysis in particular.

Myth #5

Myth #5 is that the one-person psychology that has dominated psychoanalysis needs to be replaced by a two-person psychology. The clinical insights from those schools of thought associated with the two-person psychologies have added immeasurably to the subtlety of our understanding of the psychoanalytic process. I would agree with the criticism that we have not paid enough attention to the relational components as an inherent part of the process. However, the fundamental paradigmatic shift in moving exclusively to a two-person framework (i.e., from psychoanalysis as the study of an individual's intrapsychic world to that of psychoanalysis as the study of relational configurations), in both our ways of understanding and using that understanding in the psychoanalytic method, seems unwarranted. The individual mind of the analysand needs to remain a central focus of analysis. It has been one of the basic assumptions of psychoanalysis that the patient's mind does certain things that have led the patient to

treatment (e.g., inhibits, punishes, etc.). Psychoanalytic thinking has been based on the assumption that there are central
unconscious thoughts and structures that dictate the
individual's ways of being in and experiencing the world. Thus,
we expect that analysands will react with anger or humilia-
tion to certain tendencies in others, or create omnipotent fantasies as a reparative measure, or attack in anticipation of being attacked. We believe that there are thousands of mental
acts that allow analysands to think or not to think about things
in a particular way that have led them into treatment. Unless
the analyst is willing to make some attempt to understand the
patient's mind, and comes reasonably close to doing so (especially with regard to those ways of thinking that brought
the person into treatment), a primary component of what has
led to the patient's unhappiness will be ignored.

The concept of a structured unconscious mind allows for
the understanding of certain phenomena (e.g., unconscious resistances) that are difficult to explain in other models, except
descriptively. Further, the notion of an unconscious structured
ego leads to clinical considerations revolving around distinct
models for when, how, or with what the analyst intervenes,
based on a continuum of degree of consciousness, that are
different from those treatment models that don't have such a
construct. It also leads to important differences in how the
analyst views the vehicle for change via modifications in the
ego versus the analyst's management of the interaction.

As a summation to this point, and as an introduction to
what will follow, let us look at Renik's (1995b) recent article
on the analyst's self-disclosure. Renik's theoretical justification

for the necessity of the analyst's self-disclosure is primarily with the deconstructionist point of view, captured in Singer's (1977) comments that "what the analyst so fondly thinks of as interpretations are neither exclusively nor even primarily comments about their clients' deeper motivations, but first and foremost self-revealing remarks" (p. 183). This is contrasted with what Renik characterizes as the prevailing view among American analysts that argues against self-disclosure, based on the precept that "the more a patient is presented with realities about the analyst, the harder it is for the patient to acknowledge his or her transference fantasies" (Renik 1995b, p. 473). While Renik and I may disagree on the degree and type of self-disclosure necessary for the benefit of the analysand, I believe there is nothing inherent in the structural model that prevents self-disclosure.

My own clinical experience matches Renik's with regard to the inevitable role of the analyst's enactments in an analysis where both participants are deeply involved (although we would probably disagree on the frequency with which this needs to occur). How does an expanded view of the role of the ego in the clinical setting help us understand what might be best for patient in such situation? As is discussed throughout this book, my understanding of the structural model leads me to see the greater freedom of the patient's ego (to be aware of his or her thoughts and feelings) as one of the primary goals of analysis.

Within the areas of conflict that bring the patient to treatment we see an ego frozen into rigid, repetitious ways of seeing and living within the world based on ancient but still active fears. The 40-year-old successful businessman who comes to analysis because of his anxiety and fawning ways around men in more powerful positions unconsciously believes without a doubt that these men will abandon, humiliate, or castrate him if he threatens their position. It is only by first noting the signs of resistance, that is, the holding back of a thought, his mind going blank, and the undoing of an aggressive thought, that we begin the exploration of the patient's fears, and the contribution to them from numerous sources.

A key goal of the psychoanalytic method, then, is the expansion of the ego, so that previously hidden fears and fantasies that dictated its activities as predictably as the moon's gravitational pull upon the tide are now knowable, leading to the inevitability of action being replaced by the possibility of reflection. Within this context, the patient's accurate observation of, for example, the analyst's unwitting steerage of the analysis in some personal direction not in the best interest of the analysand cannot, in most cases, be left unacknowledged. How do we invite patients to explore seemingly threatening areas of their mind, with the promise of an expanded capacity to think and feel linked with the expectation of greater freedom from their symptoms, and then suggest that certain thoughts that might be painful to the analyst are off-limits? If patients are making accurate observations about a piece of the analyst's behavior that is deleterious to the analysis, the observation itself cannot be analyzed. Patients' reaction to their observation, on the other hand, can be analyzed. Especially in those cases where the patient's ability to observe the analyst's derailment of the analytic process is the result of the work of analysis itself, it does more damage to the patient's capacity to continue to engage in the work by denying the reality of its work (i.e., the patient's increased freedom to observe and comment on the analyst's errors), than any gain that might be attained by trying to maintain some form of anonymity.

It has been my impression that many patients grew up in a situation akin to that in "The Emperor's New Clothes": systematic traumatization of the ego's emerging autonomous function frequently occurred. Children's observation of the sadism in the mistreatment they receive to "teach them a lesson" must be negated to avoid retaliation and to keep the love object. In such a situation the analyst's inability to acknowledge the reality of some piece of hostile behavior unknowingly carried out is frequently experienced by the patient as retraumatization. This issue, the role of the traumatization of the ego's emerging capacities as part of the patient's symptomatology, is not recognized frequently enough. The alcoholic father telling his daughter that his bottle of scotch is medicine when she knows differently, or the sadistic father who presents himself to the community as one of its moral pillars, is the fare of most analyses. The distorting effects of such histories on the patient's ego, with the resultant difficulty in determining what is real, let alone what is harmful, pose a formidable resistance in any analysis. Helping patients to the point that they can see we are making an analytic mistake, and then telling us about it, can for many patients be a remarkable achievement. To not acknowledge the reality of their perception in such a situation is to blunt just those capacities we have been working with them to develop.

In summary, then, the analyst not disclosing in certain situations directly contradicts one of the major goals of contemporary structural theory—the expansion of the ego into areas of thinking and feeling that previously needed to be kept from awareness. Thus, I would see nothing inherently contradictory to the structural model in the analyst being self-disclosing in certain situations. Why it has seemed this way has much to do with how the ego has been previously viewed by proponents of the structural theory. On the other hand, it is my belief that much is lost when an ego psychological perspective is not included by those theories presented in opposition to the structural model. Contemporary views of the significance of the ego for clinical technique pose an important challenge to all current methods of understanding and interpreting the clinical interaction. At the same time it offers a path toward integrating some elements of these seemingly disparate perspectives.

As I have written elsewhere (Busch 1995a), in articulating an ego psychological perspective it has been useful to isolate and study certain clinical variables. This sometimes gives the impression that key clinical issues are not attended to with this method. Yet, I believe my clinical technique is richly informed by a number of perspectives that give depth to understanding of patient communications, and by an appreciation of the numerous components in the relationship that make treatment viable or not. For example, in working with a narcissistically bombastic patient, the effectiveness of my interpretive work is dependent, in part, on my ability to absorb and contain preemptory ways of behaving while maintaining a generally positive emotional connection with him. His ability to use my interpretive efforts will be correlated with my capacity to avoid extruding unpleasant affects in the form of interpretations. Thus, for long periods of time I have to sit with the feeling of being used as a functionary or as a part of himself, as the fears and anger underlying this position can be tentatively approached in displacement.

This capacity to contain a whole host of feelings and fantasies unconsciously attempting to be actualized by the patient, so central to the ultimate effectiveness of the treatment, was first effectively addressed by those more associated with the beginning of the two-person psychologies (e.g., the school of British object relations: Bion [1959] and Winnicott [1986]). They have helped us realize that every moment of an analysis is the result of a complex negotiation of the patient's understanding with the analyst's understanding to find that workable surface that is emotionally acceptable to the patient and that brings some hope of ameliorating suffering. Our empathic attunement with what is best for the patient is the glue to which our interpretive work bonds if it is to have an effect in a deeply meaningful way. On the other hand, how and what we empathically interpret is limited by our knowledge of the human psyche. My focus on the ego and the various ways it can be usefully thought about in the interpretive process has been one aspect of this puzzle. In attempting to further define an ego psychology, I have omitted other components of the analytic process for expository purposes. This same style will be followed throughout the book.

A further word about my approach in this book. To explicate my thinking, I will occasionally turn to representative theorists from other perspectives as a sampling of key perspectives rather than as an exhaustive summary. Because I believe in the significance of small differences, I find it more helpful to characterize a particular theoretical position by representative views of individuals. It sharpens differences. Inevitably, though, major contributors to the pertinent controversies are slighted. With this regret in mind, I hope that increased clarity will result from the method of presentation I have chosen.

I have not included a review of the Kleinian perspective, in that Schafer's 1994 article has served a purpose similar to mine, although with less emphasis on the absence of an ego psychology as part of the Kleinian clinical technique. Further, my views are similar to those on the relationalists, interpersonalists, and self psychologists, which, with repetition, begin to sound like another psychoanalytic mantra.

What I hope the reader will come away with is an appreciation for how an ego psychological perspective, when added to the analyst's understanding of technique, allows, via the analysis of conflict, for the patient's greater freedom to safely think and feel what was previously unavailable to awareness. It is the basis for structural change at a deep, emotional level. Finally, I see the book as part of a conversation. Our understanding of the role of the ego in clinical technique is far from a closed book. Further, there is nothing in my critiques of other perspectives that I am unfamiliar with in my own struggles to be a good-enough analyst. Any overstatements for the technical position I espouse is, I believe, out of enthusiasm and not zealotry.

2

A Diminished Role for the Ego

Gray (1982, 1994) and I (Busch 1992, 1993, 1994) have both discussed Freud's difficulty in fully embracing the clinical implications of the structural model, and how this reverberated throughout our history of understanding technique up to the current time. However, this issue has never been addressed in the work of the two major interpreters of the structural theory over the last thirty years, Arlow and Brenner. I believe this issue is important in understanding a particular way the ego is diminished in their view of clinical technique. In one sense the differences I will be addressing may seem churlish, given the enormous contributions of these two authors to the psychoanalytic literature at large, and to the topic of ego psychology in particular. Yet, these differences have had a profound effect on our methods of understanding and intervening in the clinical situation, and deserve to be aired. Until this is accomplished, significant differences in approach to clinical material may erroneously appear to be only nuances.

From one perspective, no psychoanalysts have contributed more to the vitality of the structural model over the last three decades than Arlow and Brenner. Beginning with their 1964 monograph, which, for many analysts, finally clarified the clinical phenomena that led Freud to replace the topographical model with the structural model, while also demonstrating shifts in thinking when the structural model was applied to such areas as dreams and psychosis, their contributions to the application of the structural model have covered a vast array of clinically meaningful subject matter, including the ubiquitousness of compromise formations in psychic life, an expanded view of signal affects, the persistent effect of unconscious fantasies in all areas of psychological functioning, and the elaboration of specific defenses. In fact, it is difficult for most analysts to imagine functioning as analysts without the advances to the structural model proposed by Arlow and Brenner. The sheer magnitude of their contributions can best be appreciated with an overview of their work (Kramer 1988, Richards 1986), although there is now another decade of continual output that must be integrated. Their venerated status shall remain based on an ability to understand and articulate a complex, subtly nuanced view of psychoanalytic data in a crisp yet comprehensive manner. While my clinical understanding is often guided by their clinical wisdom, it is in the application of understanding in the clinical moment that there are differences that need to be investigated.

It has not been sufficiently understood that the work of Arlow and Brenner involved a significant departure from the beginning ego psychology of the 1950s, especially in the area of clinical technique. This ego-psychological perspective, which investigated the unique role of the ego in psychoanalytic technique (see Chapter 4), was rejected based on Arlow and Brenner's views that too sharp a distinction was made in this work between the conflictual and nonconflictual spheres of ego functioning, and that clinical analysis could not support a distinction between ego and id (Richards 1992). It was Richards (1986) who presciently stated, "It is conceivable that Brenner will eventually articulate a model of the mind in conflict in which the interpretation of the elements of conflict is such that the traditional concepts of ego, id, and superego become superfluous" (p. 11). Arlow has also come to this position (Richards 1992). In short, Arlow and Brenner have rejected the clinical utility of a separate structured ego. In contrast, I return to the perspective of the ego psychology of the 1950s, which sees understanding the ego's separate structural components as crucial to understanding central aspects of the interpretive and change process of psychoanalysis. It is a position that suggests there is clinical utility in comprehending the deeply rooted functions associated with an ego structure.

One way to highlight the differences in clinical technique between these two perspectives is via a series of questions: (1) Are there special qualities of the ego, and its place in the psychic structure, that lead to specific techniques in interpretation? (2) Do these same qualities play a role in the nature of how we view the change process in psychoanalysis? (3) Can one see resistances in operation in the patient's use of the method of free association, and is it possible to interpret these without invoking the underlying content resisted? (4) Are there important advantages to highlighting resistances without bringing in the underlying content? (5) Are there changes in the way the analyst listens to the patient's use of the method of free association with the ego at the center of clinical technique?

These questions will be taken up in depth in this and subsequent chapters, but as a summary of our differences I would answer all the above questions in the affirmative, while Arlow and Brenner would not. At its heart our differences are based on distinctive views of the ego's capacity for autonomy from the drives, and the validity of the analyst clinically separating out resistances in the patient's use of the method of free association. It leads to significant differences between aims and goals of technique.

The conceptual heart of Arlow and Brenner's method of intervention is the destabilization of the equilibrium among the forces of conflict (Arlow 1987, Arlow and Brenner 1990, Brenner 1994). That is, in their view of the interpretive process, the analyst puts before the patient ideas that have been warded off, and the patient's response to the unwelcome ideas is viewed as similar to the way the patient responded to his or her own unwelcome ideas. In this model, if the analyst believes the patient is showing an unconscious feeling, the analyst confronts the patient with it. It matters less what one disturbs than observing the ego as it attempts to restructure the compromise formation that has been destabilized. It is a view of an analytic intervention as a type of psychological cyclotron based on Brenner's oft-repeated view that whatever a patient says and does is a compromise formation and nothing that a patient says and does is just a defense. It is a very different model of intervention from one that includes the role of the ego using the structural model and Freud's second theory of anxiety (Freud 1923, 1926). As we shall see, the main difference is that in Arlow and Brenner's position attention to the ego does not come until after the intervention has been made, rather than being a prime determinant of the timing and nature of the interaction.

One of the ego's main functions, as a determinant of what is allowed into awareness, is bypassed if one believes one can intervene anywhere in the conflict rather than with what is most available to the patient's consciousness. What Arlow and Brenner suggest is the exact reverse of what an ego-psychological approach would dictate. In their view, one deals with the threat to the ego after the interpretation of the compromise formation. For them, the resistance is what comes after the interpretation of the compromise formation. An ego-psychological approach dictates one's needs to take into account the state of the resistance before making an interpretation. The ego is constantly monitoring the analytic process to determine the degree of threat. The patient is capable of using that which is not too threatening. Therefore, the analyst needs to take into account that which is knowable and work at reducing levels of threat as much as possible to manageable levels. Evidence of the patient's feeling under threat is knowable by patient and analysis via the method of free association. Thus the work of analysis becomes easier for the patient, and his or her ego becomes more involved in the process, if the experience of threat and the reasons for it are first understood before the rest of the components of the compromise formations are investigated. As captured pithily by Schafer (1983),

> There are many moments in the course of an analysis when analysands seem to dangle unexpressed content before the analyst. These are moments when the analyst is tempted to say, for example, "You are angry," "You are excited," or "You are shamed." But if it is so obvious, why isn't the analysand simply saying so or showing unmistakably that it is so? To begin with it is the hesitation, the obstructing, the resisting that counts. [p. 75]

Arlow and Brenner have never fully embraced the significance of the autonomous ego functions. Even in their classic
work on the differentiation of the structural from the topographic model (Arlow and Brenner 1964), while highlighting Hartmann's (1939) postulation of these functions from
birth, the ego is also presented as the "executant" (p. 34) for
the id in early development. In its most recent form this same
perspective is presented by Brenner (1994):

> There is no special rational part of the mind that takes real-
> istic account of external reality without being motivated by
> the libidinal and aggressive wishes of childhood, and the
> unpleasure associated with those wishes. There is no part that
> is mature, integrated, and free of conflict, as the structural
> theory assumes is the case. [p. 478]

As we shall see, the technical implications of this position re-
verberate throughout Arlow and Brenner's method of clinical
intervention. It is in contrast to an ego psychological approach,
where an attempt is made to include the autonomous ego functions every step of the way.

With their view of the ego developing as an "executant" of
the drives, we see that Arlow and Brenner seem never to have
fully embraced the thinking of Hartmann and Rapaport with
regard to the autonomous ego functions. There is now an
enormous of amount of data in support of the autonomous
ego concept, including numerous studies that show the infant,
hours after birth, with certain rudimentary ego functions, and
studies demonstrating how cognitive functions such as language, perception, and the development of thought are

prewired, leading to consistent stages of development across cultures. What the analyst actually sees in clinical psychoanalysis are significant variations in the degree to which the analysand's ego is influenced by conflict and trauma, from totally to not at all. In fact, analysts believe that an ego partially free from interferences is required for the analysand to hear, understand, and integrate our interpretations. In a starker example of how we rely on the patient's relatively autonomous ego functions, we anticipate that the patient's increasing awareness of murderous rage toward the analyst will not be followed by carnage on the highway. The notion of an ego, variously interfered with by drive derivatives, is of central importance in how we approach our clinical work.

Recent articles by Arlow (1995) and Brenner (1994) will serve as my focus for demonstrating that, in their methods of intervention, Arlow and Brenner frequently bypass the role of the ego, and my belief that there are clinical reasons for not doing so. Arlow likens analysis to an ordinary conversation, noting that unless the analyst comments on the types of occurrences that one would comment on in talking with a friend, "stilted listening" results. What Arlow means by "stilted" is close to the dictionary definition, that is, artificial and pompous.

> The mode of dress and the mode of behavior are important components of the communicative process. In the usual context of an ordinary conversation, significant deviation from the usual modes of expression would at least be noted if not commented on immediately. In treatment, when the analyst makes no comment or waits for the stream of associations

without making some comment about the changes in the patient's motor and visual communication, then the analyst is acting out the equivalent of stilted listening. [Arlow 1995, pp. 223–224]

As I have discussed elsewhere (1989, 1995b), one would get a different perspective from the view of the ego. If a patient expresses some component of a conflict via an action, it is frequently the result of a regressive ego defense taking place unconsciously. To suggest that the analyst is acting something out (i.e., stilted listening) if he or she does not comment on some change in a motor communication does not take the role of the unconscious ego into account. In fact, what Arlow is suggesting is that the analyst bypass an unconscious ego defense. For example, how one deals with a patient coming into a session with his fly open is dependent on a number of factors. It is very possible that the analyst might say nothing interpretively about it if he or she believed it was an unconscious act about which the patient had no awareness. This might be especially likely early in a psychoanalysis when the patient was unaware of, and highly resistant to knowing about, unconscious exhibitionistic wishes. The manner in which a patient dresses, looks at the analyst, walks into the consulting room, or positions himself or herself on the couch may represent complex compromise formations kept at the level of action, in part, for defensive reasons. While it may be information for the analyst, it is not necessarily intended as a communication by the patient. It is at a level of thought the patient's analyzing ego may not be able to use. This is why patients are invariably caught off-guard by comments on behaviors that are closer to actions. Doing this, we circumvent resistances that have led to the behavior remaining at an action level, where the analysand's capacity to reflect upon himself is limited.

What is important, at this point, is not so much that the patient needs to exhibit himself. Rather what one would be interested in from the side of the ego is, if the patient is having exhibitionist wishes, why does he need to be unaware of them and why does he possibly need to express them in a way that, if brought to his attention, would embarrass him. To not take such factors into account before inquiring into behavior is likely to be enacting something with the patient. If the conflict is a central one, it is likely to be shown in analysis in a form more easily usable by the patient, such as his method of using the free association process (e.g., the patient bragging about an accomplishment and then minimizing it). In working with the conflict in this manner, one is closer to what is volitionally communicated by the patient via the method we have asked the patient to work within, the method of free association. In this way we are working with an agreed-upon method, with material that is easily observable to both parties, and where the conflict might first be addressed, that is with the resistance to the expression of exhibitionistic wishes.

Our need to work in the "neighborhood" (Busch 1993) the patient is in, is one that has frequently been ignored in the literature. How one views this says a lot about how the analyst views the purpose of interventions, the goals of treatment, and the role of the patient's participation in the process, concisely summed up by Gray: "The therapeutic results of analytic treatment are lasting in proportion to the extent to which, during the analysis, the patient's unbypassed ego functions have become involved in a consciously and increasingly voluntary co-partnership with the analyst" (1982, p. 624). Further, it has been my experience that if the analyst's purpose in working less inquisitively than Arlow suggests is explained, the patient does not have the experience (predicted by Arlow) of the analyst listening in a stilted manner. For example, the analyst explaining such things as why he may not answer questions immediately (i.e., as being in the patient's best interest that the analyst listen to questions within the context of the patient's associations), leads most patients to appreciate the analyst's serious attention to everything the patient says.

I would disagree with Arlow (1995) that a prototype for the analyst's response patterns should be guided by the principles of ordinary conversation. For example, in discussing a patient's lateness Arlow states, "In ordinary conversation, one would always want to know what happened, and this would be followed by, 'And what were you thinking about keeping me waiting? How did you feel about my expecting you?' " etc. (p. 225).

From an ego psychological perspective, if a patient is late, we would wait to see what the patient did with this. Would he or she ignore it, or give a preemptory explanation about a reality event that may well have played a role in being late, or would he or she begin to associate to it? From this perspective we are waiting to see what the patient is going to do with the lateness. I simply would not feel I knew, before the patient began to associate, from which side the ego was capable of taking on this issue at this moment. Thus, to ask the patient, "What were you thinking about keeping me waiting?" is to assume that the patient's main target in being late was the analyst, and further that he or she is capable at that moment of being aware of some motivation directed toward the analyst. How would one know a priori that the patient's main purpose wasn't an unconscious, masochistic wish to get the analyst to aggressively pursue him or her?

For patients prone to feeling badgered, one might wait before bringing up issues of chronic but slight lateness. My own judgment as to what was the most salient motivation for lateness, and whether the patient had any chance of using this perspective, would have to wait for the patient's associations. Rather than seeing this as stilted listening, most patients experience this as listening carefully and respectfully to everything the patient says and does, given the establishment of an agreed-upon analytic frame. This frame rests on a free association model in which the analyst's "aim is a consistent approach to all the patient's words, with priority given to what is going on with and within those productions as they make their appearance, not with attempts to theorize about what was in mind at some other time and place" (Gray 1992, p. 324). Arlow's method bypasses the ego's participation in the process. This may need to be done at certain times in the treatment, but should not serve as a model of treatment if one sees consideration of ego factors as crucial in the treatment process. As we shall see, where one stands in relationship to this process says a great deal about the conduct and goals of a psychoanalysis.

Arlow's (1995) assertion that if something strikes the analyst as "interesting, unusual, suggestive or whatever, he or she should feel free to pursue his or her curiosity" (p. 226), seems to bypass many analytic questions about the place of such a perspective within a technical stance informed by the structural model. For example, if the analyst is very curious about something the patient has mentioned and the patient isn't, are we seeing an inhibition of the patient's curiosity? Might this first be spoken to before the analyst bypasses it? Might we not wait to see where the patient's associations lead?

From the side of the ego, one would respect patients' needs to keep themselves uninterested in their own thoughts as a regressive, defensive stance that was an adaptation at an earlier time. For the analyst to indulge his own interests, while patients are inhibiting theirs, is to bypass this potentially important disparity. The analyst's noting his or her curiosity is one thing, but expressing it to the patient without putting it into the context of the patient's entire associative process seems shortsighted. In fact, as shown in the following vignette, Arlow sometimes demonstrates a surprising lack of faith in the associative process. A supervisee is working with a patient who is becoming increasingly aware of his feelings of deprivation and anger following the birth of a sibling. The patient starts the hour by recounting how, on the way to the session, he was thinking angrily about some favored treatment given a colleague and competitor. He then mentions not being able to look at the analyst when walking by him. Arlow (1995) notes that the statement passed without comment by the analyst at the time, and throughout the rest of the session. Arlow believes such a statement is unusual enough that it would not have escaped comment in an ordinary conversation. Later in the session the patient said to the analyst, "I put you in a box and keep you separate from my other thoughts" (p. 225). Arlow again notes that the analyst didn't comment on this figure of speech, which he believes would have elicited a comment in ordinary conversation. In another example, he points out that patients say, "Sometimes I think I am in analysis for your sake" (p. 125). He believes such a statement is irrational, unrealistic, and illogical, deserving further inquiry.

But what could the analyst have said to any of the above? He might have commented on the vague but obvious connection between the patient's feelings about his colleague and his inability to look at the analyst. Or the analyst could have inquired further about any of the comments Arlow feels is worth noting. However, isn't it more important for the analyst to wait and see what the patient does with irrational, unrealistic, illogical statements before any inquiry is made? Isn't this the very heart of the associative process? We wait to see what patients do with their thoughts as an indication of how they are able to deal with their conflict? If patients are making irrational, unrealistic, or illogical statements and not commenting on them, this is ultimately information that patient and analyst might use together as an indication of something important occurring in the treatment. When patients make an associative link between their angry feelings toward a colleague and their inability to look at the analyst, I believe it is in the best interest of the analysis for the analyst to wait and see what patients do with their thoughts. For example, the patient might associate in a way that makes the link that Arlow is seeing between the colleague, the analyst, and the younger sibling more obvious. However, if the patient's associations evidence a need to undo or negate the associative link between colleague and analyst, this is important information regarding some threatening affect associated with this link. To comment on this connection in the face of such discomfort, without helping the patient see and understand first that he is showing evidence of being under threat in a way that engages his ego, is to put the patient in a situation he has already demonstrated is a threatening one.

The difference in approaches to resistances is crucial to understanding the ego as a central part of what dictates the associative process, and to understanding Arlow and Brenner's position. I believe there is evidence of the role of the unconscious resistances in all aspects of the manner in which the patient uses the associative process, while Arlow and Brenner believe that resistance is what one sees as a response to the interpretive process.

Brenner (1994) believes we can dispense with the ego, in part, because of his belief that the structural theory dictates that the ego has to do with reality and is "logical, consistent, and coherent" (p. 477), in contrast to the id. Since he believes that every perception is a compromise formation, the theory does not match the facts. However, the structural model has never dictated that the ego only deals with reality. In fact, its essence is defined by its Janus-like nature. While I will discuss this further in the next chapter, here I remind the reader of Freud's (1923) diagram in "The Ego and the Id," and this statement: "The ego is not sharply separated from the id; its lower portion merges into it" (p. 24). In his 1933 revision of the diagram (Freud 1933) the portion of the ego extended into the unconscious is even greater, with Freud reminding us, "After making the separation we must allow what has separated to merge together once more" (p. 79). Therefore, it is not clear how Brenner comes to the conclusion that the structural model dictates that the ego deals with reality, and only works on the basis of what we may descriptively call secondary process thinking.

Upon pointing out that the ego is more affected by conflict than he believes it should be, based on his reading of the structural model, Brenner (1994) comes to the conclusion that the ego can be most effectively conceptualized as a compromise formation. He believes that all aspects of conscious mental life have been shown to be a compromise formation, and that what we call the ego "is *dynamically* the same as a neurotic symptom" (p. 477).

He states, "There is no special, rational part of the mind that takes realistic account of external reality, without being motivated by the libidinal and aggressive wishes of childhood and the unpleasure associated with these wishes" (p. 478). His reading of the structural theory is that normal mental functioning is supposed to be based on a strong ego in control of the id, and since his view is that the ego is constantly affected by id derivatives, the structural theory is brought into question.

My own understanding of the structural theory is that a strong ego came to be understood as one that could flexibly integrate drive derivatives, not dominate them. (While I am discussing the structural theory in Brenner's terms, focusing on drive derivatives, the same point can be made about unconscious self and object relations.) This position is inherent in Freud's (1923) concept of neutralization and Hartmann's (1955) view of sublimation. To find an ego function driven, in part, by libidinal or aggressive wishes does not obviate the effectiveness of the function. Ambition can lead to professional satisfaction, or to taking ethically questionable actions. The ego's effectiveness is not determined primarily by the presence or absence of drive derivatives, but by its ability to integrate these derivatives into ongoing functioning. Further, the concept of an ego, more or less affected by conflict, does not obviate its importance in the clinical context. To the contrary, it strengthens it. It is our main ally in understanding what is a workable surface. For example, a patient who is tenaciously holding on to a defense has to be worked with differently from a patient moving back and forth between freely exhibiting defenses and the factors fueling it in an open, affectively expansive manner. The patient's highly defended stance must be respected, and can only be worked with from the side of its importance to the patient, if it can be demonstrated in an observable, concrete fashion. The key in these situations, it seems to me, is to find something the patient's observing ego can use to help see what is going on. For example, after a particularly moving session in which a seemingly isolated memory of his mother helped a young man understand why involvement in relationships was so frightening, he came into his next session with a series of observations about himself similar to those of a character in a Woody Allen film, that is, funny, insightful, and sometimes painful, but leaving him untouched. This was most succinctly captured in his lighthearted description, introduced with the line, "Paranoia sure can be funny," of how he felt cheated at the grocery store, when intense, brief paranoid reactions had wrecked every meaningful relationship he had begun. In this situation I felt it was important to first point out the existence of a defense in as concrete a way as possible, so that the part of him that wished to be engaged in the analysis could be utilized. Thus, I noted with him how recently we had both observed his interest in his thoughts and the feelings he had while talking about them. Today he seemed less interested in his thoughts, and he seemed to be presenting them in a lighthearted manner. This led to some productive thoughts about the defense, but my main point here is to give a brief example of how the state of the patient's ego plays a crucial role in how I feel I can approach the patient's material. Thinking of an ego variably affected by conflict is a perspective that helps the analyst know where and when to intervene in a way that is most available to how the patient is ready to work. Relegating it to just another compromise formation detracts from the important ways in which such a perspective may clinically guide us.

Brenner's (1994) dismissal of the concept of an ego on theoretical grounds has, I believe, also been evident in his clinical approach for some time. This can be demonstrated by examining one of his few, early clinical examples (Brenner 1976). In contrast to the above way of working, Brenner's method does not take into account the state of receptivity of an analysand's ego to looking at his or her thoughts as a primary consideration in the interpretive process. After a vacation, a woman returns to analysis talking of how she took up with a former boyfriend, an older man who now had a steady girlfriend. She told Brenner how content she was. One day, the patient reported the man spent more time than usual with her after having sex, and "It was so good" (p. 45). Brenner then states, "Since 'longer than he ever did before' meant more than ten minutes, I interpreted to her on the following day that she was hiding from herself her hurt, her jealousy, her loneliness, and her anger at F. for treating her as he did" (pp. 45–46). Since the patient had just told Brenner that she wasn't feeling this way, what could she do with his observation except to take it on his authority that she was wrong.

If the analyst truly believes in the meaning of a defense, he or she will not take the position that the way to get the patient to see it is to ignore its presence. The analyst needs to find some way to point out the defense that is usable by the patient and further the process, rather than contradicting the patient. In the case presented by Brenner, the patient, not surprisingly, disagrees. A week later the same scenario was repeated. This time the patient, after crying the night before about something "that had to do with F." (p. 46), reported that she wasn't upset over not hearing from him and was now over her tears. Brenner repeats the interpretation from the previous week, and the patient furiously attempts to stop him. She then left the session, slamming the door behind her. Brenner sees the patient's behavior as a confirmation of his conjecture that she is "really" angry. I see it as more likely that Brenner is dealing with a tenacious defense. The patient's response is consistent with being faced with the frightening feelings she is trying to avoid. In her mind, Brenner is attempting to put her in a dangerous situation and she reacts accordingly. If one has a model of the mind where the state of the ego's receptivity toward understanding is not taken into consideration, then knowing where to intervene is more often based on what the analyst understands rather than on what the patient can effectively use.

Part of the difficulty Brenner gets into is that he doesn't believe in the importance of defense analysis, apart from that which is being defended against, as a stage in the analysis of defenses. This is based, in part, on Brenner's (1976, 1982, 1994) views that the ego develops as part of the drives, and that nothing in analysis serves primarily as a defense. According to this perspective any interpretation of a defense needs to include that which is warded off, and one can intervene anywhere in the compromise formation. This perspective is significantly different from clinical technique based on my understanding of how the mind works. In presenting his perspective, Brenner does not see the modifications he makes from the structural model. With the introduction of Freud's second theory of anxiety, resistances were understood as the ego's response to danger. From this one can see, as clinical wisdom bears out, that it is in patients' best interest to first identify (in a way that is understandable to them [Busch 1992]) that something is frightening them, and then what it is that is frightening, before analyzing what is being warded off by the resistance.

In the case of a man in the midst of a competitive situation with his analyst, one would want to help him see first that he is anxious, and then that he is anxious over retaliation from the analyst, before suggesting to the patient that he wants to destroy the analyst and take over all his possessions. I am not saying that in some ultimate sense Brenner isn't correct. Ultimately, every resistance can be traced back to a connection with a drive derivative. But this does not mean that they must always be interpreted together.

My own clinical experience suggests that one gets much further by analyzing resistances in stages. For example, in Brenner's case discussed above, the patient may have more easily begun the exploration of her resistance if the therapist pointed out how she talks of a problem with F. (leading her to cry the previous evening), which is followed immediately by a negation (she wasn't really hurt by not hearing from him) and denial (she is now quite cheerful). I seems as if acknowledging the feeling that F. was causing her a problem was threatening. I would wonder first if she could see this flight from acknowledging a problem with F., and then, if the reply was in the affirmative, see what she could tell us about the feeling that may have led to the defenses of negation and denial. This is a different way of working. The analyst's focus is now on the danger of her feelings, not on getting the patient to see her underlying feelings. This is exactly what is being warded off. It is the feelings her anger engenders (i.e., some threat) rather than the anger per se that is warded off. Once this part of the resistance is understood, it becomes easier for the patient to understand what set of fantasies and feelings bring about the danger. Further, in the method I am suggesting, the emphasis is also on the patient's own associations as the method of understanding, rather than on some special knowledge the analyst has that contradicts the patient's own experience. The analyst brings up the patient's experience (associations), for example, the patient saying she was upset, but then undoing it with phrases like "not about" and "no longer," to examine its potential meaning, but with the focus on the defense.

Brenner has stated his position, that there are no special mechanisms of defense and therefore no special thing as defense analysis, for the last twenty years. It is an extension of his belief that the ego does not develop in isolation from or in opposition to the drives, but rather as part of drive satisfaction. Therefore, one is always looking for the other, hidden part of what the patient is doing. From this perspective, while patients may appear to be defending against something, they are in actuality doing something else. This is something that does occur in treatment. Although not described by Brenner in these terms, one can imagine that while Brenner's patient may be defending against feeling hurt by F., she might also be determinedly ignoring the transference implications as part of a sadomasochistic battle with Brenner. However, the primary question for me is what part of the conflict is most accessible to the patient in a way that will further her analysis. If the patient's unconscious wish is to engage the analyst's sadism, to bring up the patient's anger while she is maintaining there is nothing of significance going on in her relationship with F. is to enter an antagonistic, confrontational relationship with the patient that more likely than not would be an enactment of the underlying wishes of the patient. If we sensed a patient was unconsciously attempting to engage us in an action, it is the unconsciousness of the act that first needs to be addressed. As we shall see, this can often be accomplished by focusing on the patient's use of free association.

Gray (1994) has pointed out that resistances are there in treatment to be dealt with intensively on their own, and this has important implications for the ego's greater participation in the treatment. By working first with those feelings and fantasies that the patient experiences as dangerous, the ego's capacities are expanded, allowing for the greater inclusion of a wide variety of drive derivatives. To confront patients with the drive derivative at a time they are most heavily defended against it cannot be a useful technique if we take seriously the mechanism underlying defenses. Brenner's (1976) position, that in defense analysis one regularly makes reference to that which is being defended against, does not take into account the depth of feeling associated with the patient's instituting a defense. While at any one moment in an analysis there are multiple meanings to any thought or action, the fundamental question about technique is how to best plumb the full depth of the conflict. It is my impression that this is best done with patients who have a sense of safety (i.e., feeling free to explore their own thoughts), based on greater understanding of the dangers that may have kept thoughts from their mind.

Brenner's views of what happens to defenses during analysis, along with his conceptualization of what the structural theory dictates as cure, are different from my understanding of this same phenomenon. Brenner (1976, 1982) does not see defenses changing in progressive ways or becoming less pathological; rather, his focus is again more on the drives in a successful analysis and how they become less disguised and distorted. This is contradicted by what I would consider a paradigmatic example of a successful treatment, elaborated on in the next chapter. Early in treatment a patient, upon glancing at the analyst, is convinced the analyst is upset with her. At this time in the analysis, questioning the patient directly about this is, for her, like asking why she thinks someone who is seven feet tall is tall. It just is. At a later point in the analysis the patient may have the same perception, but be able to wonder if her perception was correct or might it come from her. Alternately, she might wonder, even if the perception was correct, why she might have been attuned to this aspect of the analyst. What one sees in this situation is that the patient's feelings, which previously were unacceptable to her, are now more easily available. Descriptively, what seems to have happened is that a feeling that was previously frightening to the ego is no longer so dangerous. From this perspective there has been a major change in the defense. That which was previously frightening is no longer so. There has been an ego expansion. The drive derivative is more tolerable, because of the changes in the ego.

Brenner's (1982) disavowal of the structural theory is based, in part, on his conclusion that Freud believed successful defenses led to the repressed being barred from consciousness. Yet, by 1926 Freud distinguished the defense of isolation from hysterical amnesia. Brenner passes over the distinction Freud made between a drive derivative in the form of an idea, and the availability of that idea to consciousness. Freud was clear that there is a difference between an individual having a hostile thought, and being aware of the hostile nature of the thought. It is the everyday fare of analysis for the patient to say something he or she thinks is cute or funny, which the analyst takes as dismissive or diminishing. The defensive process that allows for this simultaneous process is one that seems frequently bypassed by Brenner.

Brenner (1982, 1994) believes that what changes in a successful analysis are the compromise formations and not the defenses. It is another reason he proposes discarding the structural model. However, it is like trying to argue that the decrease in smog is not because of less carbonaceous material in the air, but because of the percentage increase of non-carbonaceous. Compromise formations change, in part, because of modifications of defense. Drive derivatives are more allowable into awareness because they become less frightening. This is an important basis of defense analysis. Brenner's (1994) view that it is the compromise formations that change, leading to the eschewal of the ego as useful concept in analysis, is based on his interpretation that the structural theory dictates that conflict disappears. "To use familiar terminology, the goal of treatment is the resolution of conflict. The ego is supposed to become stronger as well as more mature, conflict is supposed to disappear" (p. 479).

As I have indicated above and elsewhere (1995a), all the signs in successful analyses indicate that the ego does become stronger, but this is not synonymous with conflict disappearing. What changes is the inevitability of conflict *expression*, not the inevitability of conflict. Thus, when Brenner points out that symptoms persist after psychoanalysis, and uses this as an argument against the structural model, it is another interpretation of the model that I do not share. I have tried to show that the particular way patients work with the development of symptoms after a successful analysis is different from their preanalytic ways, and it remains a powerful argument for the significance of the ego in the analytic process.

As an example of how patients' defenses don't change or become more mature, a female patient is described (Brenner 1982) who, after having had sex only with women prior to the analysis, began to have sexual relations with men. While the analyst was on vacation, the patient entered another lesbian relationship. Back in the analysis the patient consciously struggled to give up the relationship, while "trying to provoke" (p. 83) the analyst. During one session the patient was arguing with herself as to why she should give up her girlfriend. There were frequent pauses during which the patient was "obviously waiting for the analyst to speak" (p. 83). He interpreted to her that she was waiting for him to speak so that she could rebel the way she had numerous times with her parents. Implicit in this, according to Brenner, since the interpretation had been made many times before, was that her anger really was about not having a penis, and that her father, mother, or analyst didn't love her as she believed they would if she were a boy. Brenner reports a dramatic effect with this intervention by the following week, leading to eight major changes he views as due to analytic progress based on properly timed interpretations.[1] However, it also leads Brenner to observe,

> A defensive identification with men was present both before
> and after the interpretation. Before the interpretation this de-
> cisively influenced her sexual behavior. She had wooed a
> woman and was engaged in a sexual relationship with her, a
> relationship in which the patient played the part of a man.
> After the interpretation the same identification was expressed
> in her vocational behavior. She took steps to become the
> pupil of the man she admired in order to learn his skills and
> to be able to use the tools of his profession—tools, it may
> be added, which had a phallic significance. [p. 86]

He then goes on to state,

> She still identified with a man. The tools of her teacher's pro-
> fession were transparently phallic symbols, and to learn to
> use them expressed her unconscious fantasy that she had a
> penis. Can one say her use of identification as a defense was
> any less infantile or more normal after the interpretation than
> before it, even though the compromise formation of which
> it was a part was certainly more mature and normal. [p. 87]

My difference with Brenner is in how we conceptualize

---

1. Puzzling in the example was that it wasn't clear what defense Brenner
thought he was interpreting. What he seems to be describing is the
patient's difficulty in knowing she is angry at Brenner. If this is the
case, it is difficult to know how Brenner's remark would be helpful
to the patient, except as beginning an investigation of why the patient might be needing to do this. What is also interesting is that five
of the changes Brenner reports are behavioral, as if these were self-
evident examples of the result from well-timed interpretations (e.g.,
discontinuing the lesbian relationship, more feminine in dress and
manner, etc.) and couldn't be due to numerous factors.

greater maturity or normalcy. I believe we are on a slippery slope when we evaluate behavior on its symbolic or unconscious meanings. Any act, when looked at from this perspective, can be seen as pathological. What we can see as analysts are significant changes between patients and their own thoughts. This is the primary way we can determine changes in defenses, and within the analytic setting one can see significant changes. It is patients' greater freedom to be aware of their own thoughts, as well as the capacity to be able to observe their observations, that characterizes changes in defenses (Busch 1994). The unconscious meaning of behavior does not change in analysis. What changes is the analysand's freedom, leading to increased capacity for gratification. It is this freedom that we expect to be correlated with new capacities outside of the treatment.

Brenner (1976), like Arlow, is an interventionist. That is, he portrays the analyst's job as directing patients toward the sources of their conflict, rather than helping patients understand those *barriers to their exploration*. He states,

> Instead of directing his attention to the task of discovering the elements of the psychic conflict responsible for both the patient's symptom and for his anxiety and guilt, he may take the latter at face value, so to speak, and follow the patient's lead in attributing anxiety (or guilt) to the symptom rather than the conflict that underlies it. [p. 12]

This is a different position from one where the patients' ego is at the center of technique, leading one to see that patients either are ready to analyze something or are showing why they aren't ready, which is just another step in the process of analyzing. It isn't that I would never suggest an active intervention; it is just that the analyst-as-interventionist model is antithetical to our understanding of the role of the ego as monitoring degrees of safety. If a patient comes in talking of a symptom as due primarily to external causes, it is not our job to direct him to the internal causes. It is our job, based on the associative process, to try and understand the barriers to seeing an internal conflict, including the patient's bedrock belief that his symptoms aren't his own. While Brenner is obviously interested in the internal meanings of behavior, he gives the impression of analyzing symptoms, behaviors, and actions rather than focusing on the patient's productions within sessions. As I have tried to indicate above, by keeping one's eye more on the associative process the analyst is in a better position to judge what the patient is ready to·work with. If there are resistances to seeing a piece of behavior as part of analytic scrutiny, this is the issue for the analyst to keep in mind.

A point frequently overlooked is that it is unconscious threats that lead to unconscious resistances. For example, a male patient in the midst of an oedipal struggle with the analyst literally fears that his penis will be cut off if he challenges the analyst. In such a situation one is dealing with a regressed 5-year-old ego, characterized by thoughts being closer to actions and only an intermittent ability to reflect back on one's thoughts (Busch 1995b). To point out the unconscious wish to defeat, challenge, or conquer the analyst in such a situation will certainly bring about an intense reaction. However, it will be the reaction of an endangered, beleaguered ego, hardly ready to look at his reaction as anything other than a reality danger. This is why, in my readings of the literature, so many analyses are conducted within an atmosphere of hostility. The analyst is attacking patients' basic sense of safety by prematurely bringing to their attention thoughts and feelings that are experienced as dangerous, without first helping patients see that they are feeling under some degree of threat, and what the threat is about. Thus, patients react as anyone would who is feeling under threat.

Kleban's (1994) depiction is typical:

> Again the compromise formations in the transference had shifted. As her defenses were analyzed she felt more anxious and guilty about her underlying impulses toward the analyst. She felt panicked and helpless and tried again to withdraw from this awareness. At the same time, however, she began to openly express hostile aggressive feelings in the transference for not being gratified by the analyst. [p. 441]

What Kleban describes is a reaction a patient often has when asked to bypass defenses, without understanding why they are there in the first place. Raphling (1992) captures this position when he states, "Interpretation, in order to convey insight, of necessity *assaults* or challenges patients' psychic equilibrium" (p. 354, italics added). It is my belief that when the analyst interprets defenses, taking into account the patient's feeling of danger, while analyzing why this particular defense was chosen and its adaptational nature, the process of defense analysis is not fraught with fear and anger. If the feeling of threat can be brought to the patient's attention in a way that allows for the use of more mature ego functions, this gives just enough distance to the patient's experience that the mixture of the patient's ability to both experience feelings while also reflecting on them is greatly aided.

What seems to be frequently forgotten is that, in areas of conflict, the ego is in a perpetually regressed state. This is why we need to find ways to involve the more mature components of the patient's ego functioning in the analytic process, and why respect and appreciation for this side of the patient's ego is so crucial for analytic progress. Gray's vision of the analytic process as an increasingly voluntary copartnership with the ego, and the success of the analysis as dependent on not bypassing ego functions, speaks to this component of the analytic process. The ego's regressed state also has ramifications for the manner in which we interpret to patients. It is important to note (due to the regressed nature of the ego) the concretistic nature of the patient's thinking in the midst of a conflict (Busch 1995b), and how the analyst's interpretive style must be geared toward this type of thinking (Busch 1995b, 1996, 1997). The analyst's comments are being heard by an immature ego, and unless we can speak in a way that is understandable to such an ego while also enlisting the efforts of more mature ego functions, our efforts will not be relevant, with the attendant consequences varying from patient to patient.

The resistance most uniquely the patients' is the myriad ways they react to the threat of their unconscious material coming into awareness. It is the hesitation, avoidance, negation, undoing, focusing on the present versus the past, and so on, that are the patient's living responses to the dangers the ego unconsciously perceives in the scanned thoughts, actions, or feelings. What Arlow and Brenner describe as the resistance is the patient's response to the analyst disturbing the equilibrium of the compromise formation in a particular manner. At its most basic it is a response to another person (the analyst) attempting to bring what is threatening into awareness without taking into account patients' feelings of being endangered. What Arlow and Brenner bring about with their method is an interpersonal reaction, which is different from patients' intrapsychic reaction to their own thoughts.

In summary, Arlow and Brenner have presented a particular model of working clinically that has been consistent over the last thirty years. In their model all mental functioning is viewed as based on compromise formations, with the ego's formative development dependent on its role as executant of the id. The analyst's main task is to bring central components of the compromise formation to the attention of an essentially passive ego. This will lead, inevitably, to a variety of intense reactions as patients are faced with what has been threatening to them. The approach I am suggesting is based on a different view of Freud's second theory of anxiety, and the role of the autonomous ego functions. In what I would consider an approach based on ego psychological principles, the resistances are what one pays attention to before an intervention, not after. Further, the ego's participation, and especially the more autonomous ego functions, are a necessary part of treatment from the beginning. The ego's capacity to work with the analyst's intervention is a key component of the method. While the words Arlow and Brenner use to describe methods of working may, at times, be similar to ones I might choose, in practice the methods can be quite dissimilar.

3

The Expanding Role of the Ego

From session to session, within each session, and from analysis to analysis, the psychoanalytic clinician is dealing with fluctuating ego states. This can be observed in clinical phenomena such as the following:

1. The degree to which the patient is open to thoughts and feelings coming to his or her mind;
2. The degree to which certain thoughts and feelings are more available to the patient than others;
3. The degree to which a patient is open to the thoughts and feelings that come to his or her mind as a potential statement of a psychological state;
4. The degree to which a patient's thoughts and feelings are an attempted actualization of a conflict; and
5. The degree to which the patient is open to understanding the psychology of his or her own mind.

A patient coming into a session saying, "I was thinking in the waiting room about my old girlfriend from high school," can be the beginning of a reflection on why this thought came to mind, or a reverential memoir on the girlfriend's multiple charms. Each is a psychological statement, but the patient's availability to see each as a psychological statement will vary. An ego-psychological approach adds to the psychoanalytic clinician's perspective by highlighting the significance of a careful monitoring of the patient's capacity to understand and utilize an intervention in a cognitively and emotionally meaningful manner, and the ways the analyst functions that may foster or hinder this process, as a central component of treatment. The patient's increasing freedom to use his or her own mind is viewed as both a beacon for intervention and a necessary part of the change process. Thus, from a contemporary ego-psychological perspective changes in clinical technique revolve around the way we listen and interpret. It involves closer attention to the patient's use of the method of free association, using a number of considerations to guide us, and finding a workable surface as a basis for interpretation. New understanding of the importance of the ego's participation in the analytic process has led to these changes, which will be spelled out in detail in the remainder of this chapter, along with the rationale for considering the ego a crucial component of the change process in psychoanalysis. What is offered is a perspective, not a handbook. While this perspective will serve the psychoanalytic clinician to clarify ways of working, it will not interfere with the mystery and complexity of the process.

I begin this chapter with two clinical examples as a demonstration of my perspective. While no single example can serve to fully illuminate a clinical point of view, I offer these first vignettes because in my discussions of them with colleagues they seem to capture one aspect of the shift in perspective offered by a contemporary ego-psychological approach. They are presented as an introduction to a way of working and understanding that will be elaborated throughout the rest of this chapter.

The patient, Dr. A., a physician and married mother of two who had been in analysis for a year and a half, came from a family where she was treated with casual neglect and occasional physical abuse. The treatment to this point had revolved around our growing appreciation for the degree to which her internal life was taken up with feelings of mistreatment as a beginning explanation for the sense of being "beaten down by life," which brought her into treatment.

Dr. A. began the session with a familiar set of complaints about not being treated well by the office staff in her group practice, feeling they were not offering efficient support in billing and record keeping. It was not unusual for her to begin the session in this way (i.e., someone was not treating her well).

How I hear such a beginning is contextual, depending on a wide array of variables. It is what allows me to sort out the multiple meanings potentially inherent in this opening. Is it a reference to the state of the transference? Is she asking for my support for the difficult situation she feels herself to be in? Is she asking me to provide a function that no one was able to in her growing up, that is, the protector she didn't have? Am I being forced to passively accept her view of the situation? Is this a regressive retreat from a more active, affirmative stance? There is no single way to think of such a moment, and my various hypotheses encompass structural conflict, a self-psychological deficit, and a relational perspective.

My understanding of the rhythm of Dr. A.'s sessions was that she often began in this way, but it was with vastly different affective shadings. At times she was coldly insistent on her view. At others it was more like hearing a friend tell a funny story about a misfortune many years before. You can hear the pain in the story, but with time the feelings aren't so raw and the existential absurdity of the event is now primary for the storyteller. Today, Dr. A.'s beginning to the session was told in a slightly self-mocking tone. My understanding of it was that she was still seeing things the same old way, but was able to look upon it with some amusement. To this point there is nothing particularly unique to an ego-psychological perspective. Rather, it is the kind of listening we all do to orient ourselves to the full range of what the patient is presenting.

Dr. A. then recalled an incident that had occurred the previous evening. She was doing some professional reading at home when her husband called to her saying that their son needed help with his homework. She told him she was busy, and asked if he couldn't help him. He did, and later the two of them had a pleasant discussion about vacation plans. This series of events was told with an air of pleasure and slight wonderment. It was the kind of situation where, in the past, Dr. A. would have immediately put down what she was doing to help her son, and felt resentful at what she saw herself being forced to do. Alternatively she might have told her husband, in an irritated fashion designed to raise his ire, to take care of it himself. However, her brief flirtation with pleasure in her actions quickly turned into denigrating self-mockery, with a dollop of criticism mixed in. "Big fucking deal," she said, "I'm 42 years old and can get my husband to help me out."

This is an important moment in the session where there is an observable shift from the patient taking pleasure in effective action to a masochistic retreat. As patient's thinking in the midst of conflict is concrete (Busch 1995b), a moment where a regression, based on an unconscious conflict, is played out right before us is an ideal time to try to engage the remaining observing ego in an exploration of the conflict (Gray 1994). Something just happened (i.e., a conflict, not immediately consciously available to Dr. A.), which led the patient to retreat to self-denigrating behavior, a central part of her character. It is moments like this the ego psychologist hopes to capitalize on by focusing on what might be most observable and understandable to the patient's ego at the moment of an active, unconscious conflict. It is a most effective way of engaging the ego, and there are vast differences among us as to how much this becomes central to our technique.

I noted how Dr. A. had shifted from pleasurably discussing how she had taken care of herself in a way that allowed others to also help her, to becoming self-critical. She was intrigued, and then a memory came to mind that she hadn't thought of in years. She was about 6 or 7. She and her little sister had gotten up earlier than her parents. Dr. A., thinking she would let her parents sleep longer, decided to feed her sister breakfast and watch cartoons with her. Then her mother came downstairs and complained bitterly about the mess she had made in the kitchen, and she felt crushed. I commented how, today, when she starts to talk about taking better care of herself, she begins to attack herself, as if she were now compelled to do to herself what was once done to her.

In first noting the shift with the patient, I prefer to see what part she is able to respond to. Others look to the moment before the shift occurred, but I believe it may be more useful to follow the patient's lead on this. What is lost in the specificity of the moment is gained by the belief in the patient's use of the method of free association. While the patient's going to the past may be a resistance to a deeper exploration of the feeling immediately before the defense occurred, it is still a useful window into a defense. There is no one component of a resistance that is a key, and anything that sheds light on it is useful analytic information. I also try to stay closely tied to the patient's associations, whenever possible, rather than listening more impressionistically (Busch 1997).

Dr. A. briefly hesitated and wondered if she was telling me the whole story. She knew she presented what had happened as her helping out. She wondered if there were other, more sinister factors going into her behavior. Didn't she really know that she had left a mess? Was she trying to win over her sister's affection, proving to her mother that she was a better mother? How could we know that she was a victim and not a perpetrator? We've seen this other side to her also. She gets uncomfortable when I appear to take her side too much. I wondered if her discomfort was because I was wrong, or because I took her side. With some hesitation she noted she felt a lot of pleasure when I was talking before, and it was not only what I was saying. The familiar timbre of my voice was also comforting. She noted that talking about this was making her very uncomfortable.

I told her I thought this was an important observation in that it seemed to serve as a trigger for self-critical feelings.

Here we see Dr. A. begin with a continuation of a masochistic regression. What allows me to present a perspective on the sequence of associations the patient seems unaware of? Her view is that we are missing what a hostile person she is, while I am suggesting something different can be seen in the sequence. Primarily my intervention here is based on my reading of the therapeutic alliance, by which I mean the patient's capacity to step back from the affective component of his or her thoughts and feelings to use that part of the autonomous ego that is open to psychological observation. There are times in a treatment when patients are so caught up in the truth of their perception or affect that there is little the analyst can productively question. Yet there are times in treatment when patients are ready to consider their thoughts, even the most affectively charged ones, as psychological statements. It is at these times, I believe, that the analyst has more latitude in approaching the patient. However, distinguishing between an inquisitive ego and one that is surrendering to a higher authority is not always easy to determine at the moment, but can be evaluated over time.

In this first vignette I have demonstrated one component of a contemporary ego-psychological approach, as I understand it, which highlights the close process monitoring emphasized by Gray (1994) within a contextual framework. Shifts in associations are paid attention to as potentially observable demonstrations of conflict that utilized the patient's observing ego as part of a philosophy of treatment that champions inclusion of the more conscious components of the patient's ego as a necessary part of the change process. However, shifts in association can only be understood within a context of empathic understanding, and is not something that can be applied automatically.

This next vignette demonstrates the significance of considering a structured mind in our interpretive efforts.

I had to change an appointment time and asked the patient (a 35-year-old woman who came to analysis because of depression and multiple inhibitions, currently in her second year of analysis) about an alternate time. She agreed to the change in appointment time, and after a brief pause, started to cry. She then began to berate herself for crying, saying, "It's really stupid." In a dry, unemotional voice, she elaborated on how she was momentarily feeling bad that she would have to miss an aerobics class to come to the appointment, and this is what led to her self-reprocess. (Her enrollment in aerobics was a recent development after never having exercised.) She thought it was stupid to think of an aerobics class as being more important than therapy. It reminded the patient of her previous therapist, who, when exhorting her to come more frequently to therapy, suggested she should do anything she could for her mental health.

This led to a thought about how bad she felt over the weekend. She had come home from work on Saturday, and started eating. (She is a petite woman.) She had popcorn, then some cocoa with buttered toast. It reminded her of her childhood, and how much she liked this combination as a child, especially when she dipped the bread in the cocoa. She spontaneously explained the reasons why she had used butter rather than margarine, citing a recent newspaper article regarding use of corn oil–based margarine and its negative effects, matching those of butter. In this, it seemed like the patient was speaking to an anticipated reproach. Her thoughts then turned to going out for dinner the previous evening, where she ended up ordering not what she wanted but what she thought would be healthiest. The meal was not to her liking. I reminded the patient of how the session began, resulting in her inhibiting a feeling (crying), and becoming self-critical. Her thoughts then went to situations where she seemed to feel what she wanted was excessive, followed by attempts to curb her appetites. This suggests she inhibits herself because she feels what she wants is too much, too excessive, and too indulgent.

The patient then associated to having sex with her husband the previous evening. In an unusual display of assertiveness, she suggested to her husband that she would be interested in intercourse. This was also unusual in that the patient rarely wanted or obtained pleasure from intercourse. According to the patient, her husband gave various reasons why this wasn't a good idea, that is, she doesn't enjoy it, by the time she put in her diaphragm she wouldn't feel like it, and several others. He was right. By the time he was finished talking she had very little interest in any type of sexual pleasure. Her thoughts then turned to a time when she was 3 or 4, when her mother came into her room when she was rubbing the nap of her flannel sheet and sucking her thumb. Mother changed her sheets to cotton the next day. These had a whole different feel. She had difficulty sleeping after that, and has had continued problems. I said, "You feel you have a long history of having physical pleasures disapproved of, and that you shouldn't care about giving these up. This sheds further light on your initial reaction of berating yourself for your sadness over giving up aerobics."

The patient's thoughts then turned to the mess she has at home, and the constant dilemma she has about cleaning up. Has she ever told me about this touching phobia she has? (She hadn't.) There are certain textures that she just doesn't like to touch. Crisco came to mind. She hasn't used that in years. Recently she surprised herself when using something with a similar texture, and she was sort of getting into it. As she's thinking about this, she's aware that she's feeling anxious. It reminded her of the time her daughter first got Play-Doh, and they both really got into it. Funny, she doesn't remember her daughter playing with it much after that.

In the first part of the session just reported, the patient interrupts her crying, berates herself, and then has a series of associations in which she felt bad for indulging her needs, resulting in an inhibition (i.e., eating what she thought she should rather than what she wanted). My interpretation is based on this sequence. In hearing this material, colleagues frequently respond by asking, "Isn't she really crying about the change in appointment time?" or "Isn't she really angry, and turning her anger against herself?" While these considerations are important to keep in mind, they speak to core issues regarding how we as analysts understand clinical material, and the workable surface. While many writers have attempted to capture the surface at which the analyst might best work— my own "in the neighborhood" (Busch 1993), and Levy and Inderbitzen's (1990) "analytic surface"—Paniagua's (1991) conceptualization of a "workable surface" seems the most apt description. Paniagua noted how the analyst is always working with three surfaces: the patient's surface (i.e., that which the patient is immediately conscious of trying to communicate); the analyst's surface (i.e., the amalgam of thoughts, feelings, and fantasies the analyst has that lead to a variety of speculations regarding aspects of the patient's psychology in what he or she is communicating); and the workable surface (i.e., the space between the first two surfaces usable by the patient's ego in the change process). Another way of describing the workable surface is that it is that combination of the patient's thoughts, feelings, and actions, and the analyst's reaction to these, that is usable by the patient's ego. No matter how brilliant the analyst's reading of the unconscious, or how empathic the analyst is with the patient's underlying feeling state, it is most often not useful data until it can be connected to something the patient can be consciously aware of. Monitoring accessibility to consciousness, along with delineation of interpretive strategies based on this variable, is a central part of treatment guided by the concept of a structured mind.

The focus of my interpretations is the inhibition that occurs right in the session, while it is the feelings that *trigger* the inhibition, rather than what is *behind* these feelings, that seem most important at this point. It is the moment the patient needs to inhibit her crying, rather than what caused her to cry, that is my immediate focus. These two levels of inquiry often get mixed up in our clinical thinking. If it is correct that what she is really crying about is the analyst's request for a time change, and some feeling this stirs up in her (e.g., feeling discarded, insignificant, etc.), analyzing the conflict over *wanting* is a crucial component of this process. How can the patient know that she really wants the analyst to keep the regular time, while the conflict over wanting remains unanalyzed? While we as analysts believe we are interpreting more deeply by getting behind a feeling, from the perspective of the patient it will frequently end up being more of an intellectual exercise. For this patient, which is deeper—an assumed feeling she is defending against, or the recognition of an inhibition in action (both in the session and her associations) with lifelong consequences, which was a symptom that brought her into treatment in the first place?

After my initial interpretation the patient's associations led to current and genetic components of her inhibition, as well as dynamic-genetic suggestive content (i.e., anxiety over the wish to play with feces). It is the deepening of the associative content, as well as its internal consistencies, that lend weight to the correctness of the initial formulations.

In addition to those techniques that characterize attempts to use a workable surface (e.g., focusing on observable inhibitions), there are multiple ways of evaluating the patient's readiness to consider what he or she is doing in the analysis as a psychological statement at any one moment. This is another component of what makes a surface workable. At certain points in treatment we can predict when a patient beginning a session with a dream will herald readiness for new insight into an ongoing investigation, and when it will be the opening salvo in the patient's feeling misunderstood and hurt when his or her efforts are not appreciated. In the former case we have far greater latitude in determining the workable surface than with the latter, where even the most tactful approaches to the reasons for presenting the dream will embroil the analytic pair in disagreement, which makes the finding of a workable surface more complicated.

Some patients might begin a session in a lifeless manner, with thoughts presented in fits and starts, which characterizes one type of patient in a highly defended state. At some point in the session the patient may reflect on what has been occurring: "I wonder why I'm in such a muddle today." Such a statement may be a harbinger of a shift in the patient's relationship to his or her own thoughts, and may be followed by a greater ease in talking and coherence of content. This portends a different workable surface from that of the patient who retreats to further self-recriminations. Slight shifts in affective coloring, as when words change from being potential barriers to exploration (e.g., insisting, imploring words) to vehicles for exploration, also suggest a change in the workable surface. In short, I see the concept of a workable surface as a dynamic, flexible one, encompassing the multiple variables analysts use to evaluate the level at which patients are ready to engage with their analytic productions. It is based on the degree to which there is an observing ego (Sterba 1934) able to deeply engage with a psychological mind. It a useful variable for the psychoanalytic clinician to keep in mind as a guide for how we engage the clinical material. The patient aching for a fight needs to be approached differently from one attempting to understand his thoughts as psychological statements.

In my conceptualization of the affective component of an ego psychological perspective, the analyst is constantly evaluating the patient's affect tolerance in determining what is most available to the patient's ego. This is what we mean when we describe interventions based on the degree of threat to the patient, which is at the center of resistance analysis. While I have primarily emphasized the patient's use of the method of free association (Busch 1994, 1997), this is not listened to in isolation. Determining when a patient's movement from direct references to the analyst should be thought of as a resistance and when it is an elaboration in displacement involves a necessary empathic attunement if interventions are not to become routinized. Further, regardless of one's technique, there simply must be considerable empathic attunement in order for another human to feel understood. Technique is only useful when applied empathically.

Our ability to be attuned to patients also comes through in the timbre of our voice, the words we choose, and many other signals, in addition to the particular content we speak to. One can point to how an expression of a feeling was followed by its opposite in a mechanized fashion, or with a sense of interest, curiosity, and compassion. Whether the patient experiences the analyst as involved or intellectualized depends a great deal on the manner in which the analyst communicates his or her interventions. From another perspective, the analyst must absorb and contain a number of affects and ideas as he or she follows the associative process while waiting for a workable surface to emerge. An underappreciated component of psychoanalytic work is the necessity to sit with a variety of emotions and ideas while following the patient's associations, waiting to understand that component of a conflict the patient is most able to reveal and understand. It may not be possible to interpret a narcissistic patient's defensively cancelling a session shortly before the analyst's vacation, as there may not be anything available to the patient that would lead him or her to understand this as a plausible explanation. The destructive hostility the analyst may feel at these times must be absorbed, as he or she attempts to work with safer areas for the patient's ego. It is in this way I understand the application of Bion's (1959, 1962) concept of containment, and Winnicott's (1960) holding environment.

One is never working in a clinical vacuum. With most patients there are, for long periods of time, issues in the foreground and issues in the background. With the patient discussed above, whose appointment time changed, her inhibition in and out of the sessions was increasingly palpable. The degree to which it affected the quality of her life was becoming clearer. We had been working on the edges of this issue for some time, and increasing feelings of freedom along with regressive retreats had become regular parts of the analytic landscape. If the patient's not associating to transference was part of a long-standing sadistic dismissal of the analyst, then its absence might be handled differently. I am mentioning this simply to acknowledge the importance of the clinical context in our interventions.

But why consider the ego at all in our interventions? In response, I will present a couple of clinical vignettes as an introduction to my basic premise—that a major change process that takes place in a successful analysis is based on an *expansion of the ego*. With this expansion, what previously could not have been thought about or felt now can be, while thinking itself becomes qualitatively different. This, then, has critical implications for technique.

Early in an analysis, a patient, upon first seeing the analyst when entering the consulting room, believes the analyst is mad at him. The patient's conviction is such that for the analyst to ask him what led to this conclusion often leads to incredulity (e.g., "Would you ask me why I think the sun is shining?"), or a description of what he saw in the analyst's face (e.g., "You had a frown," "Your eyes seemed mad") that led to this inescapable conclusion. At a later time in a reasonably successful analysis the same observation could occur, but this time the analysand might ask the question, "Why might I have seen you as angry?" or "Why did I pay most attention to what seemed like an angry look on your face?" What has changed? First, there has been a change in the level of thinking, from thought that remains concrete and cannot turn back upon itself, to thought that can take itself as its own observation. Thinking that was regressed has become more mature. Second, a feeling that previously was unacceptable as potentially originating within the patient is now tolerated and able to be owned as part of the experience. Put another way, the patient has become less defended against awareness of a feeling within himself.

The change that occurred in the patient in this vignette involves an expansion of the ego in two ways. Thinking that was constricted and limited to the concrete has opened up to the potential for greater abstraction. Also a feeling that was unacceptable to the ego, leading to the initiation of a defense, is now more tolerable to it. The ego's capacity to tolerate this feeling has been expanded.

An analyst is a few minutes late for an appointment. When the patient begins the session, her thoughts may be blocked, or she may go into a tirade about traffic, or she may place the analyst in an idealized position. At a later time in the analysis, the patient could become aware of feelings or irritation with the analyst and say something to him.

What has happened is that a feeling that was previously experienced as dangerous, either to know or talk about with the analyst, is now available for the patient to experience. The patient's fears are less fearful. Where previously the analysand was limited in what she could allow herself to feel or think, these thoughts are now available to consciousness. An analysand in a successful analysis can comfortably feel and think about considerably more of what she is thinking and feeling.

The above vignettes characterize an important part of the change process in psychoanalysis. The results of psychoanalysis are not rooted in conflicts changing, but in *modifications in the ego* that allow analysands to think about conflicts differently. The dangers previously associated with certain thoughts and feelings are no longer so fearful. Thus what one expects to see in a relatively successful analysis is a greater freedom of thought (Kris 1982), and changes in the analysand's capacity to reflect on her thoughts and feelings. That which was previously experienced unconsciously, and reacted to on that basis, can now be brought to consciousness and reflected on. Follow-up studies of successful analyses (Pfeffer 1961, Schlessinger and Robbins 1983) reflect this process. Previously analyzed patients, upon meeting an interviewing analyst for the first time, will demonstrate the central conflicts that were worked through in their analysis. However, over time, the active demonstration of these conflicts will dissipate, reflecting the re–working through of the conflict.

Characteristic of thinking caught in conflict is the compulsion to act, because conflicts and their solutions are initiated at a time when thinking is closer to action (Busch 1989, 1995b). However, as the frightening affects and thoughts are allowed into awareness, more primitive ways of thinking (closer to action) give way to higher levels of thinking (e.g., self-reflection). From this deceptively modest accomplishment, the inevitability of action gives way to the possibility of reflection. This, in turn, has profound implications for the individual's ability to control rather than be driven by conflicts. Structural changes have occurred in the ego that have led to basic changes in what analysands can think about and in how they can think about what they think about. This is what Loewald (1971) suggested as the curative process of psychoanalysis, whereby experiences and feelings previously repressed now come under the influence of higher level ego functions. The one modification I would place on this is that it isn't that previously feelings and experiences are necessarily repressed, but rather that they are under the sway of an ego that is functioning in a regressed manner. Thoughts and feelings do not have an "as if" quality but rather seem real, much as they do for a child waking from a bad dream. What changes is the capacity to experience these thoughts and feelings differently.

Another way to conceptualize the ego modifications that occur in a successful analysis is within the context of a developmental theory of the mind. Mayes and Cohen (1996) review the growing cognitive developmental literature that demonstrates a developmental line for an increasingly sophisticated capacity for representation and perspective regarding the child's own world as well as her relationship to it. "These processes are also part of basic capacities such as understanding the separation between one's own mental life and that of others and between psychic and external reality, . . . and appreciating the relationship between wish and action, impulse and deed" (p. 118).

Mayes and Cohen present the following example of a limitation in taking into account the perspective of the other, which has relevance for my perspective on the change process in psychoanalysis. A 3-year-old observes a child come into a room, put down a doll, and leave the room. Another person then comes into the room, moves the doll, and leaves. When the child returns to the room, the 3-year-old is asked where she will look for the doll. Invariably the 3-year-old answers that the child will look for the doll where it has been moved to, rather than in the original spot it was placed. "She is apparently unable to understand how her own beliefs can be different even momentarily from the external world as she now perceives it" (p. 128). What changes over time is "the capacity to take the perspective of the other or to appreciate the other's mental world even if it contradicts with his own" (p. 129). This capacity is relevant to the clinical examples just discussed. It is another way of looking at a developmental change that occurs in the ego during psychoanalysis that accounts for the patient's changing perspective on her own thoughts in relation to the other. Thinking that was previously limited to a self-absorbed perspective can now take into account the other. It is similar to, but not the same as, changes that occur in a patient's relationship to her own thoughts.

In short, what I have described are basic structural changes in the ego that lead to modifications in how patients think about their feelings and thoughts in terms of what is allowed into awareness, who is the initiator of thoughts, and how one can think about one's own thinking. These are elemental factors in the psychoanalytic change process. If one accepts the validity of the ego's centrality in the change process, clinical guidelines follow that then distinguish an ego-psychological perspective from other methods posited as representing techniques based on the structural model. Before presenting these guidelines in detail, I will summarize the differences between what I am suggesting as a contemporary ego-psychological perspective and what has been presented previously as representative of clinical technique based on the structural model:

1. The ego functioning of analysands is highly variable. They might have disastrous love relationships, but at the same time they often hold responsible jobs, successfully raise children, in some cases treat and help their own patients, and so on. The transforming effect of analytic understanding in the midst of intense transferential reactions is an example of the rapid shift in ego functioning occurring within an analytic hour. In fact, we rely on that part of the ego that remains relatively intact and autonomous from conflict to make use of our interventions. Yet, we have seriously underestimated the necessity of including the patient's more autonomous ego functions as part of the analytic process. Ways of working that capitalize on and foster ego autonomy lead to revisions in what we interpret and how we interpret.

2. Central to a contemporary ego-psychological perspective is resistance analysis based on the premise that resistances need to be interpreted as part of an adaptation to a persistent, unconscious threat. The resistances can be observed concretely in the patient's use of the method of free association. This is in contrast to those methods that view resistances as most observable after compromise formations have been confronted. Most theories of technique seem not to appreciate the crippling effects of resistances on the ego, and rely on extra-analytic methods to overcome them.

3. Closer scrutiny is paid to the patient's use of the method of free association. The patient's associations are seen as adaptive compromises, with our methods of intervention chosen to highlight the ego's participation. This is in contrast to those methods that see the patient's use of the method of free association primarily as a superhighway (but not quite a royal road) to the unconscious, while the analyst's ego functioning (i.e., what he is making of the associations) is at center stage. In fact, as we shall see, the trend in psychoanalysis is increasingly toward less attention paid to the patient's use of the method of free association, especially when the analyst's subjectivity is championed.

4. Common variables receive fresh insight when looked at from a contemporary ego-psychological perspective. For example, action, rather than being seen as just another form of communication, can be understood using the concepts of ego regression and ego arrests (Busch 1995b). As noted earlier, how the analyst uses his own thoughts and feelings as part of the psychoanalytic process can also be looked at fruitfully from the side of the ego.

In this brief summary I have tried to highlight specific ways a contemporary ego-psychological perspective differs from previous views of methods based on the structural model and other techniques. It is part of an ongoing elaboration. The remainder of this chapter fills in the details.

If one considers expansion of the analysand's ego as a ma-

jor component of the change process in analysis, certain perspectives on the analytic process become clearer. The ego described as Janus-like (Freud 1923), with one part turned toward, and a piece of, the inner world of the unconscious, and
another part directed toward the outer world, depicts how all
conflicts are mediated through the ego, and new understanding of them must come through the ego. Connection to the
inner, unconscious world must be made through that part of
the ego that is turned toward the outer world, that is, the part
that thinks of itself as logical and rational. However, these
functions of the ego have never become seriously integrated
within clinical technique, which has been documented with
regard to the unconscious ego resistances (Busch 1992, Gray
1982).

I have tried recently to look at the ego's mediating function and its consequence for technique (Busch 1996). Using
the basic method of the psychoanalytic process (i.e., the
method of free association), it becomes incumbent on the
analyst to speak to what is most observable to both parties
(i.e., the patient's use of the method of free association) in
order to demonstrate the existence of conflict and the resistances to observe it. As Gray (1994) has noted, one of the
most powerful means to demonstrate an unconscious resistance
is in the context of a patient's diversion (in speech or thought)
from an associative pathway. Using the ego's power of observation, we provide powerful, verifiable evidence of a current
conflict being expressed, outside awareness, that is playing a
significant role in the patient's thought processes. Compare
this with the more abstract method of hypothesizing an un-

conscious resistance based on an absence of a thought or feeling (e.g., the ubiquitous interpretation of "You must have been very angry" when the analyst hears a patient talk about a situation that the analyst believes would make many people angry).

My technique is based on the premise that destabilizations of compromise formations inevitably occur in the context of any relationship, leading to the expression of its various components. As noted earlier, this is a very different view from that which currently guides technique according to our current understanding of the structural model. In broad brush strokes the task of the analyst is to create an atmosphere in which the patient's conflicts can be freely expressed, while finding a way to approach, observe, and explain them so that the ego's participation can be enhanced. In general, this requires paying careful attention to those internal factors that have led to ego restrictions (i.e., resistances), while finding ways to discover and understand conflicts that further the ego's participation in the analysis rather than restrict it.

I have written at length (Busch 1995a, 1996, 1997) on ways of thinking about technique from the perspective that one must approach the unconscious ego through that part of the ego that believes and highly values its own rationality. In general, it involves speaking to patients about their conflicts, and using data that make sense to them. At the same time it requires an approach to patients and their thoughts that is not infantilizing. From the beginning of an analysis there are ways of dealing with patients, their thoughts and feelings, and the analyst's thoughts and feelings that make the whole process less mysterious and authoritarian, while encouraging the ego's participation. These ways include a full explanation of the basic rule and involve the role of resistances. I try to stay closely tied to the patient's thoughts, and use them with the patient as the basis of my intervention.

After finding myself withdrawing in angry silence from a patient, I realize that he has been dismissive of most of what I had been saying the last few sessions, but within an overt context of friendliness and cooperation. His thoughts never deepened; they appeared instead as a series of isolated events. He noted the paucity of his thoughts. I then remembered various associations he had been having of older rivals being shut out, the most obvious one being where he noted how much fun it would be for his mother to visit his new apartment, and for them to spend the day together walking around town. In his thoughts his father wasn't included, although he was also visiting.

A key moment in these associations is when the patient shows the capacity to observe a resistance in action (i.e., the paucity of his thoughts). At this point there has been some shift so that his capacity to observe his own thoughts has widened. I first wait to see what the patient is able to do with his observations. In this instance he struggled with allowing anything to come to mind. Using the patient's brief moment of increased observational capacity as a guideline, I noted his difficulty in allowing thoughts to enter his mind, and suggested this might be a continuation of his observation of a "paucity of thought." What I noted, I told him, was that while his manner seemed friendly, there were a number of occasions recently when he became dismissive. I gave him some examples and then wondered if his difficulty in knowing more about his thoughts had to do with an uneasiness with the emergence of some not-so-friendly thoughts. Before going any further with the interpretation I would wait to see if he was able to utilize this interpretation of a resistance.

This is in contrast to a case mentioned by Arlow (1979): After a female patient complained about sticky, smelly stuff used by her beautician, and workmen who had left her apartment dirty and damaged, the analyst asked the patient: "Are you menstruating?" While Arlow links this question and the associated thoughts with the patient's central feelings about herself, it is irrelevant to the issue of whether the analyst should have intervened at that point in that way. If the patient is needing to hide the fact that she is menstruating and feeling bad about it, this is what might be most helpful to start with if there is material that comfortably allows for the patient to understand this. Also, in what way does it further the analytic process for the analysand to know that the analyst can glean from her associations that she is menstruating? Without at least sharing the basis for his observation, and the reason for his bringing it to her attention, the analyst is asking the patient's ego to take a subservient role to the analyst's ego capacities. How is the ego involved except as an admiring observer? I believe with Friedman (1989) that "psychoanalytic treatment does what the ego does" (p. 536), and that we cannot expect the patient to bring a necessary intelligence to the process if we don't make it intelligible. Too often overlooked

is how much we need to rely on "old-fashioned causal, explanatory, correlating, rational intelligence" (p. 546) as part
of the process. Otherwise, we keep the ego excluded from the
process, which, of course, works in a diametrically opposed
direction from those changes that seem to define successful
psychoanalysis, for example, expansion of the ego.

As I wrote previously (Busch 1994, 1995a,b,c, 1996), part
of relying on the patient's intelligence involves working with
and intervening at the level of what is most immediately knowable to the ego. While based on clinical experience, and supported by knowledge of ego functioning, backing for this
position also comes from the burgeoning field of cognitive
psychology. Schacter (1996) reports that a certain type of
learning experience, "elaborative encoding" (p. 45), promotes
higher levels of what we can remember while increasing the
richness of our memories. This type of learning is dependent
on integrating new information with what is already known.
In describing the incredible memory of chess masters, Schacter
notes,

> After just a five-second exposure to a board from an actual
> game, international masters in one study remembered the lo-
> cations of nearly all twenty-five pieces, whereas novices could
> remember the locations of only about four pieces. . . . But
> when the masters were shown a board consisting of randomly
> arranged pieces that did not represent a meaningful game
> situation, they could remember no more than the novices.
> [p. 48]

This is a powerful example of the effect of contextual meaning upon memory. The use of information is inhibited when

it is given without reference to previous context or meaning. It is a point I will be returning to many times in this monograph.

The necessity of the patient's regression has been considered an important component of the analytic process. The standard reason given for this has been patients' need to fully experience the power of their more primitive feelings and accompanying fantasies to understand the depth to which these feelings have been ruling their life. While I agree fully with the necessity for analysands to experience this more primitive side of their self, it is inaccurate to say this is the result of regression. What has not been sufficiently appreciated is the degree to which patients arrive in analysis with their ego already in a regressed state. The careful, restricted forays into the methods of free association typical of neurotic patients is the result of an ego in a regressed state. Their whole manner of thinking, as I have indicated at length (Busch 1995a), is the expression of an ego in a regressed state. These patients, who may be admired for their creativity and productivity in their professional life, when invited to delve into areas that brought them to treatment, become narrow and stereotypic in their thinking. It can only be this way, in that when these patients enter the area of their neuroses, they come upon thoughts and feelings that are perceived as dangerous. It is only after the unconscious dangers have begun to be understood that patients can enter into previously walled-off areas of primitivity. Thus it is a regression with the aid of an expanded ego capacity that allows patients to experience their more primitive side.

In fact, much of the interpretive work I hear about from colleagues encourages the patient's passivity and a reliance on the analyst's belief system. While encouraging expansion of the ego in terms of unconscious content (although not the unconscious resistances), the process of intervention rarely includes the patient's ego as part of the process.

Here is an example from Greenson (1967) that is typical of a type of work I have frequently heard about.

> In the first year of his analysis, a young man comes into a session angrily denouncing a professor who lectures "without thinking of whether the students can follow." As he continues in this vein, he slips and says that he hates "to have him treat—I mean, teach me." He then challenges Greenson with the comment, "I suppose you will make something of that" (p. 299). When the patient continues to complain about the teacher, the analyst asks him, "Aren't you trying to run away from your anger toward me?"

This is a typical example of what I described above, and a type of resistance interpretation that is frequently made. Why Greenson thinks the patient is really angry at him and why he thinks the patient is resisting this remain unspecified. It is left to the patient to accept Greenson's interpretation on faith, or some unarticulated link to his own experience. However, it is just this experience that the patient has indicated he is feeling some need to retreat from, and he is ready to get into it with Greenson about just this type of interpretation: "I suppose you will make something of that." To include the ego as part of the process, we might say to the patient, "When you made the slip that indicated there might be some connection between your feelings of anger toward your professor and me, you needed to undo it, and seemed ready to get into it with me about the possibility of a connection. I wonder what comes to your mind about what makes such a connection noxious."

Greenson and I are in agreement regarding the feelings the patient is having in a displaced fashion, and the resistance to seeing this. Greenson's method bypasses the patient's resistance to seeing his anger at Greenson ("Aren't you angry at me?"), while taking up a challenge the patient made ("I suppose you will make something of that") and forcing either a fight (which the patient may be happy to engage in with Greenson at this point, thus relieving him of the burden of what he is angry about) or acquiescence. The patient briefly takes the latter route, but then returns to criticizing the professor for being a big shot who "doesn't give a shit about me." Greenson intervenes at this point with the comment, "Aren't you angry with me for going on my vacation next week?" Now Greenson adds to the interpretation a cause for the patient's anger, which there seems to be even greater resistance to than the feeling itself, since the possible references to being left are even more disguised. However, even if the patient had learned from Greenson's interventions that he was angry about Greenson's vacation, he is left completely in the dark as to why he couldn't know about this. The part of his psychic makeup that led to this restriction in the ego remains untouched.

Why the feeling and its associated content is threatening to the patient remains unknown to him. This aspect of his con-

flict, the explanation of which would have important applica-
bility for other situations, remains untouched. The patient is
left with an intellectualized thought that he is bothered by
Greenson's going away. His fear of knowing that this angers
him, and why this is fearful, remains unknown. This is a typical place where many analysands end up in their analyses. They
have a general intellectualized idea that certain kinds of key
events in their lives have led to certain conflicts. They have
many explanations for their behavior, but no understanding
of the unconsciously experienced threats that keep the more
primitive feelings and fantasies from coming into awareness.
It leads to the type of stereotypic explanations of conflict one
hears in second analyses, such as anniversary reactions, sibling
rivalry, problems with competition, and so on.

The problems with the manner in which Greenson works
were pointed out by Searl (1936) some sixty years ago. Un-
fortunately, her insights into the problem of working in this
manner remain excluded from general clinical technique. By
telling patients what they are thinking (e.g., "Aren't you really angry over my vacation?"), Searl (1936) notes that we do
not help them with their inability to know this themselves,
and leave them dependent on the analyst for self knowledge.
By implicitly telling patients it is a fantasy or feeling that is
the cause of their ignorance of what they are thinking or feeling, as in the example above, the analyst implies it is knowing the fantasy or feeling that leads one to not know things.
"The dynamics of the patient's disability to find his own way
have been comparatively untouched if the resistance was more
than the thinnest of crusts, and will therefore still be at work

to some extent and in some form whatever the change brought about by the interpretation of absent content" (p. 479).

An ego-psychological perspective views the patient's associations as constructions that are a result of the ego's monitoring thoughts, often unconsciously, for the degree of risk they pose. This is a very different model than the patient's verbalizations representing wolves (unconscious) in sheep's clothing (Freud 1905). Another way of putting this is that in a contemporary ego psychology the associations are viewed as a text with an organic unity to it that will express the conflicts and the compromise formations they have led to. The analyst works close to the patient surface, with the belief that this is all the patient can tell at this time. Further, the closer we are to the surface, the more understandable our interventions are capable of becoming for the patient. This is also an important part of technique, that is, keeping in mind the ego's ability to participate as one component of how and what we interpret. The analyst's most brilliant interpretation means little to the patient if he or she is not ready to hear it.

This is a different model than our current ego psychology, which is highly investigative and confrontational. It is my experience that if one has faith that, in the associative process, the patient will tell as much as he or she can use at the time, then the analyst as the initiator of the process becomes less prominent. In our current model the analyst is the stimulus for change via an interference with the compromise formations. The model I am suggesting sees the end result of the associative process as the determiner of what the patient is most able to understand at the moment. The analyst listens to patients' associations to hear what they are warding off, thinking about, or trying to communicate. One's interventions are geared toward what patients are most able to understand, presented within the context of what is observable to them in their use of the associative method.

A middle-aged man, trapped in what he felt was a loveless marriage, was increasingly becoming aware of how much he looked to be mirrored by others, especially women. He was approximately five minutes late for one session, which was unusual for him. As he began the session, his associations were both about reasons for his being late and questions about whether he was late at all. Then he realized that his stopping to talk with a female co-worker had led him to be late. This led to a highly intellectualized set of thoughts about a particular dynamic we had talked about earlier in the treatment regarding the relative significance of the men and women in his family. He then mentioned a one-minute differential between his watch and my clock, seemingly given as an alternate explanation for why he was late. This is good example of an observable conflict in action. The issue of his lateness is approached, and then negated. It is helpful to patients in their understanding of unconscious conflict if it can be shown in observable form. This is not a hypothetical conflict. It is one that is openly expressed in the patient's associations.

I said to him that he seemed to be having difficulty taking a stand as to whether he was late or not, and both giving explanations for why it was so while raising doubts as to whether it was the case. He now realized that he was making an argument for why he wasn't late, as our clocks had different times, even though he knew it wouldn't account for the amount of time he was late. His thoughts then went to a list of topics he wanted to argue about, including lateness, dreams, and slips. He then described how each time these came up he felt forced to look at them, and bemoaned the fact that he couldn't simply ignore them if he chose to. He gave a plausible argument for how focusing on these issues was an interference with the method of free association. He then wondered why he was pissing and moaning about this. He knew the importance of issues like being late and slips. He had seen it many times in the analysis. I noted with him how he interrupted his argument with me, suggesting some uneasiness with these feelings as we had seen in the beginning of the session.

He then described a series of interactions with women where it seemed likely he might feel angry. He first mentioned a situation at work in which he had helped his firm disentangle itself from a complicated professional situation. One of the women in his firm had complimented him on his adeptness, but added a few comments that made his skill seem like a character flaw. Next he told of an interaction with his mother, in which it was clear he hoped for her approval of something he had done recently, but she did not offer it. He had let his neighbor borrow his VCR, which she promised to return the next day. It was now two weeks, and she still had it. His secretary at work had screwed up another phone message today. He then stopped and noted that this seemed to be related to what we were talking about, but he couldn't see how. This is a key moment when the patient's observing ego can focus on the associations as psychological data. One now has an ego involved in psychological meanings, which gives the analyst greater freedom in his interpretations. This is very different than the Brenner example where the patient was actively fighting off psychological meaning.

I pointed out to him that in response to my noting his discomfort with thoughts about arguing with me, he brought up a number of situations where women did things that might plausibly lead to his feeling angry. However, this latter part seemed to get left out, suggesting a lot of discomfort with angry feelings toward women. He realized that he guessed he was angry in these situations, but he couldn't feel it. It led him to think about a newspaper article he had read recently about a child who had been taken from his mother because of suspected abuse. A year later he seemed to be thriving, and then was killed in a spray of bullets from a drive-by shooting. I said this suggests that a part of him feels that as bad as an abusive relationship is, it is safer than leaving it. This helps us understand why, at times, he might not want to know of his anger. As I talked, he found himself thinking about the neighbor who borrowed the VCR. Specifically, he thought of a variety of plausible explanations for why she hadn't returned it, and also how everyone in the neighborhood thinks she's great. Was he too demanding? He could see how difficult it was to keep even a mildly critical thought in mind.

This is an example of working with the patient's associations, seeing them as either an attempt to defend against or illuminate a particular conflict. By staying near the patient's associative flow, one is staying connected to an observable surface that is available to both parties to go over and see what can be gleaned from it. The patient begins with a demonstration of a conflict (i.e., difficulty in letting himself know he was late). Using a descriptive portrayal of his use of the method of free association, I could point out his conflict in an observable fashion. In his thoughts he then demonstrated one of the factors in his resistance, that is, uneasiness with his angry feelings toward me. This then led to associations regarding his mother and other women where he needs to defend himself against awareness of his anger. Pointing out the defense against the awareness of feeling angry in the context of an expanded observing ego leads to an unconscious fantasy that to become aware of his angry feelings is to leave a relationship and die.

The theory of technique was rooted in Freud's discovery of the unconscious at a time when energy transfers were seen as paramount in bringing about a cure. Thus anxiety was seen as being due to dammed-up libido, and psychic evacuation of the derivative impulses was seen as the cure. It remains an active model in psychoanalytic technique. Getting to or at the unconscious drive derivative remains a primary analytic goal, with interest in why it remains hidden. What may be the best way to help the patient understand its existence is of less interest. While not eschewing the significance of unconscious derivatives in psychic life, it is best to pay attention to those factors that lead to the unconscious derivatives being kept out of awareness, and finding ways to speak to this and the emerging derivatives that is easily understandable by that part of the ego that is capable of understanding our interventions.

In this context, I believe we need to pay more attention to the text as written by patients, that is, their use of the method of free association. I am convinced that many of my colleagues listen for what is hidden by the associations rather than for what can be read in them. Usually this is done in some "sign" fashion, where the analyst believes there is something of importance that should be on the patient's mind (e.g., an upcoming vacation, the transferences, a feeling, the patient's cancellation), and all thematic content gets squeezed into this perspective, whether the analysand is ready for it or not (e.g., the Greenson case cited above). This is in contrast to using the patient's associations as the primary text. It is the difference between seeing the analyst's role as akin to working on a jigsaw puzzle versus digging for oil. In the latter one is using clues on the surface to see what is buried underneath. In the former one works from the position that all the pieces to the puzzle are on the surface, so it is a matter of finding the best way to put the puzzle together. As Searl (1936) noted some sixty years ago,

> I believe that only when one abandons the attempt to deal directly with absent content and with truly unconscious material—or at least when one tries to do so—does one become aware of the wider possibilities of analytic work which lie hidden in the conscious and preconscious material. . . . This work of putting things into places to which they belong, making true wholes and separating false ones, can be more

effectively carried out, I believe, if the analyst keeps his own work in the place to which the patient allows that it belongs—voluntary expressed material. [p. 484]

My assumption is that, given the proper instructions in beginning analysis and without undue influence from the analyst, patients will use the method of free association to the best of their ability, that is, they will be willing to tell us as much as possible of what is on their mind up to the point when there is too great a threat to the ego, and they become threatened either consciously or unconsciously. Thus, I see patients' associations as a text to be read rather than unraveled. I try to work with the surface of what the patient has told me, based on the notion that this is what is safest for the patient to bring up. Interpretations are based on the ego's capacity for observation. Other sources of information (e.g., the analyst's fantasies or feelings) are most effectively used by the patient when they are integrated with what is observable within his or her use of the associative process. As I have indicated elsewhere (Busch 1995b,c), in the midst of conflict patients' thought processes are characterized by a concrete, here-and-now quality. Their ability to look beyond the immediacy of their own thoughts at the moment is limited. This is why using the patient's own associations as a vital part of the interpretive process is such an important component of technique.

Mr. M., a successful professional in his 40s, returned to analysis after the analyst's summer holiday. While he experienced the analysis as enormously helpful, it was difficult for him to translate this into any positive feeling toward me. It was symptomatic of a certain distance from which he experienced life, and it was increasingly bothersome to him. He began by noting that he had been thinking a lot about the analysis right after our last session before the break, but then felt like the press of everyday events took over, and he didn't think about it again until yesterday.

Something happened shortly after the sessions ended, and he was irritated that he couldn't talk with me about it. He learned from his friend G. that a mutual friend from graduate school was in from out of town. When he heard about this from G., he expressed his pleasure and his hope to see the friend. They made tentative plans for Mr. M. to get together with them at G.'s house on Sunday. When he called G. on Sunday afternoon, he learned, much to his chagrin, that his friend had already left town. He was outraged for a few days, and couldn't understand why he wasn't included in their plans. He realized his anger was somehow out of proportion, but found that he didn't want to let it go. In trying to understand why he wasn't included, he wondered if these guys were jealous of his successes. His thoughts then went to their sexual identity. Both had tried marriage twice, neither time successfully. G. hasn't dated for years. G.'s younger brother left his first wife for a man.

The patient then mentioned he had a dream the previous evening. He was at a party at an estate. It was my house, and we had an appointment. However, his family and other people he knew were there, and he had difficulty getting to see me. The only other person he noted in the dream was a second cousin who is gay. He then started to talk about other events that had occurred during the past two weeks with his business.

I noted with the patient how with most dreams he is able to associate to the various parts, but he had uncharacteristically left this dream without specific thoughts about it. However, I thought this was what he was attempting to describe today, that is, his need to keep his distance from me and the analytic material. I reminded him how he described not thinking about me or our work after feeling irritated when I wasn't available to talk with him about something that bothered him. The incident was one where he was kept from seeing someone who was important to him in the past. This occurred, he speculated, because of issues of sexual identity in the air. He then reported a dream in which he can't get to me, partly because of a homosexual cousin. I suggested it was difficult for him to be aware that he was bothered by not being able to see me, because this raised issues for him of someone's sexual identity (his, mine), leading him to need to keep his thoughts about me at a great distance. As he noted, hanging on to his anger at me while I was gone seemed helpful to him.

The patient then reported that the previous evening he and his wife had a brief spat. He felt her pulling away from him, and this infuriated him even more. Yet he found he wanted to hang on to the anger. He found himself having a very pleasurable fantasy of telling her he wanted a divorce. He wondered if this was similar. He realized he was fantasizing about how macho it would seem to be walking out on her and how bad she would feel. I agreed, noting that in his thoughts it was the macho thing to be the leaver while the woman was left.

I try to stay near the patient's associative material, seeing it as an organic unity that will express various components of a conflict. My method is less investigative than that of others who may also be working within the structural model. They may feel that letting a defense go by without questioning it is poor technique. Resistance analysis is equated with an aggressive attack on the defenses, with the seeming assumption that the defenses will solidify unless they are consistently undermined. Such an approach might have led an analyst to begin his or her interventions when the patient described how everyday events took over his thinking, and the analysis and analyst were no longer on his mind. However, by waiting, we can use the patient's further association to better understand the resistances and the affect. In this manner we give credence to, and show the benefits of, the associative process. It is startling to me that while we emphasize the significance of the method of free association for the analytic process, we actually use little of the process. Rather than using the associative process as a whole, analysts use it in listening for signs. The result is that many patients end their analyses unaware of, and still unable to use the method of free association as a basic staple of an ongoing self-analytic process. My interpretation was essentially a reconstruction of the patient's associations. It conveys the idea that if we listen carefully to the patient's associations we can learn a great deal. It is a model I consider essential in the patient developing a capacity for self exploration.

Silverman's (1987) published clinical sessions serve as an example of another method of working based on what I described as the semiotic method. The ebb and flow of the patient's associations are ignored for a sign the analyst seeks. From the patient's perspective, the analyst's use of the patient's association remains a mystery and becomes grist for the analyst's mill. A female patient begins a session with numerous expressions of aggression that she then needs to undo. "I've been mad at you all week. It's not that I'm mad at you" (p. 151). Then after describing being angry at her roommate she says, "It sounds so silly" (p. 151). She then describes something hostile she was going to say, but decided not to say it. We see here, in the observable use of the method of free association, the expression of a feeling and the immediate undoing of it. It is at this point we are seeing a resistance in action. This is the moment at which it is most advantageous to explore the resistance to the feeling of anger. Pray (1994) has shown how picking up on these moments, where the conflict between the feelings of anger and the defense against the feeling are easily observable by the patient's observing ego, are the heritage of Anna Freud's method of defense analysis and seen in the work of Gray (1994).

Silverman's method of working is quite different. After the patient described still another situation where she was angry (having to wait two hours at the hairdresser's), and felt she couldn't say anything, Silverman thinks, "It's the end of the week and she has to wait two days to see me again on Monday—like the two hours at the hairdresser's—and in two weeks I leave on vacation, and she'll have to wait a month for me"

(p. 152). Silverman's thoughts are on why the patient may be feeling angry, rather than helping her explore the difficulty with her knowledge of and expression of her own anger. What good does it do the patient to know she is angry, when indeed this is apparently frightening to her as evidenced by the resistances against just this feeling? Further, Silverman's analytic ear is attuned to the transferential sign meaning of the number two, while its context within the patient's full set of associations is ignored.

To return to the case, the patient then describes various situations where with various men, like the hairdresser, she becomes dumb and doesn't understand things. She links this to a lifelong pattern, beginning with her father. This appeared to be her way of expressing aggression, while remaining unaware of the intent, that is, her compromise formation. She then says, "It's the same thing here. I keep feeling like asking you, 'What does it mean?' I always feel like you know. I feel like asking you now. I know you've told me you don't know anything until I've told it to you, but I don't feel that way. You know, because you're smarter than I am and all that training and experience you have" (p. 152). Silverman then says, "I don't think that's what it is. I think you feel I know because I'm a man, that as a woman you don't have the brains" (pp. 152–153). At this point in the session, what seems like a coherent piece of the patient's conflict, expressed via her associations, is derailed.

As I see it, the patient begins the hour noting, via her method of associating, the conflict she has in expressing her aggression to Silverman. She then expresses her aggression in the way that she always has (i.e., her major compromise formation) via appearing dumb. This seems to be a central issue for this patient, clearly expressed in the associative process. One does not have to look beyond the process to delineate the conflict. Caught in his search for the symbolic meaning of the behavior, Silverman enacts something with the patient by telling her that yes, indeed, she is stupid because she thinks it is one problem and he knows it is really another. Why does he think she is wrong? Why does he think she is saying things that are wrong? What does this have to do with the rest of her associations? None of this is evident. What she has been expressing in her associations to this point is ignored, except as something that has led to an enactment. What is focused on is what the patient hasn't been expressing, that is, the absent content that Searl (1936) noted adds little to the patient's understanding of a process that can be useful to her.

The tendency to ignore the patient's use of the method of free association has received increasing currency with the championing of the analyst's subjectivity. There is a perceptible tilt, especially among relational and interpersonal analysts, toward a treatment structure focused on the analysand's needing to grapple with the analyst's personality and associations, expressed in the extreme in Levenson's (1993) view of the patient as "not only the interpreter of the analyst's experience, but a collaborator in the therapist's cure" (p. 394). This trend toward focusing on the interactional mix, while paying relatively less attention to the patient's individual mind, is another way in which we show what I believe to be a ubiquitous tendency to move away from careful attention to the patient's use of the method of free association. From another perspective the awareness of the subtleties of the analytic relationship has been greatly expanded by the relational and interpersonal theorists.

Unique to psychoanalysis, and part of its heritage from the beginning, has been the understanding of resistances to change. Freud's (1895) "pressure" technique was his first attempt to deal with this phenomenon of treatment, and while Freud's method became more psychological, resistance analysis still bears the imprint of his earliest method of overcoming resistances. Compare these two quotation, one from Freud and one from Greenson some seventy years later.

> Thus when I reached a point at which, after asking a patient a question, . . . I was met with the answer "I really don't know," I proceeded as follows. I placed my hand on the patient's forehead or took her head between my hands and said, "You will think of it under the pressure of my hand. At the moment at which I relax my pressure you will see something in front of you or something will come into your head. Catch hold of it. It will be what you are looking for. Well, what have you seen or what has occurred to you?" [Freud 1895, p. 110]

> I was aware her tone had a quality of irritability and annoyance. So after some ten minutes of this, I intervened and said, "You seem annoyed." She answers, "I guess I am, but I don't know about what." I say, "Something is irritating you. Let's try to find it. Just let your thoughts drift with the idea, something is bothering me." [Greenson 1967, pp. 113–114]

It has been well documented by now that changes in the technique of resistance analysis, supposedly brought about by the discovery of unconscious ego resistances and signal anxiety, have never been fully incorporated into clinical technique. While integral to an ego-psychological approach, the significance of resistances as an unconscious act of the ego is not shared by other clinical perspectives.

Gray's (1994) method of close process monitoring is the fullest exploration of an ego-psychological approach to resistance analysis to date. Friedman (1984) likens this process to an observer watching an experienced canoer negotiating a river. The observer sees the canoe swerve to and fro, but cannot see any obstruction. The canoer is not necessarily consciously aware of the obstructions, but is picking up signs that there is a danger to be avoided. If the observer were to bring any particular swerve to the canoer's attention right after it happened, he could more likely become conscious of the specific sign of danger. Gray's point is that the patient in analysis will suddenly swerve from a topic when coming upon an unconscious resistance. It is an observable moment that, when utilized by the analyst as a beginning exploration of the danger, enlists the patient's ego rather than bypasses it. There is a burgeoning literature on close process monitoring and its relationship to resistance analysis (e.g., Davison et al. 1990, Goldberger 1996, Holmes 1996, Levy and Inderbitzen 1990, Paniagua 1985, 1991), especially to individual content. There are numerous examples of this concept throughout this monograph, as well as questions about it.

The variety of resistances to the method of free association itself needs to be explored further. For example, resistances can take such forms as changing the method of free association into recitations of everyday experiences, focusing on problems that have occurred between sessions, describing various feeling states as intuitive explanations for current conflicts, and memories of life events as explanatory concepts. In all these cases the patient is telling the analyst something, not looking to see whatever is on the patient's mind. For example, rather than the method being used to explore thoughts as a way of understanding the significant conflicts in life, all difficulties are reduced to the patient's mistreatment by a significant object from the present or past. In one sense the patient is saying what is coming to mind, which becomes both the data of analysis and a resistance to the analytic process. However, as the method of free association and its role in the analytic process have become less clear to analysts (Busch 1994), it becomes difficult for them to effectively point out to patients, in a way they might find informative or useful, the significant resistant elements in how patients may reconce- ptualize the method of free association.

The subtleties of patients' resistances to observing their thought processes are endless. Only by the analyst working with patients via the method of free association can patients' resistance to it be helpfully pointed out. It has been my experience that once patients see the value of the method of free association, they feel cheated by their own need to remain unobservant of their own thought processes. Even brief glimpses of the method convince people of the power of their own thoughts to be harmful to them when hidden, while they feel empowered by split-off elements of thoughts and feelings becoming reintegrated into awareness. In short, looking at patients' "participating ego" at a macro level (i.e., the approach to the method of free association) can become an important source of information for analysands and analyst about the readiness of analysands to freely think their thoughts. However, it is only useful information within the context of the analyst's commitment to, and effective use of, the method of free association.

Much of the above can be seen in the following example:

A patient in the fourth year of analysis gives me a curt hello, with a furtive glance in my direction, before rushing into my office Monday morning. This is his usual Monday greeting. I have learned that he needs a lot of psychological space, but this is particularly true in beginning the Monday session. It is a feature of his schizoidal adjustment to life, which is increasingly becoming clear to both of us but shows significant signs of shifting. He begins the session by reporting that he had a dream the previous night. (This, in itself, was a recent development. Dreams were often reported later in sessions, and often given short shrift.) We were in an analytic session standing back to back. It reminded him of two people having a duel. As we were standing there, his hand touched mine and I said to him in an annoyed tone, "What do you think you're doing?" It reminded him of how he keeps on waiting to hear me become annoyed with him. He thinks he probably listens for it in my tone whenever I talk. "Why should you be seen differently?" he wondered (a reference to this as a characteristic of much of his listening to others).

His thoughts turned to the weekend. He realized he was struggling with feeling depressed, and felt it had something to do with his absence from the sessions (a distanced but important reference to his acknowledgment of his growing awareness of my importance to him). He then described how he had been thinking less this weekend about buying something to make him feel special. However, upon seeing an older man getting out of an old BMW that had been lovingly cared for, he found himself thinking about getting a similar car. He had been mad at drivers all weekend. He then stopped his narrative with the realization that, while he felt he was telling me about things that were meaningful, there was a particular way he was doing it that didn't feel quite right. He was telling me what he *had* thought, rather than telling me what he *was* thinking, even if it was about what he had thought. He didn't catch it until just now. He suddenly remembered that on the way over he was looking forward to coming in, but then imagined getting into an argument with me about something. Was this why he was talking this way? He sensed there is a certain way he is not giving credence to his thoughts. Was he attempting to draw me into a fight? Now that he can see it, he thinks he probably was. It fits with his thoughts coming over here. Why does he need to do that?

I then said to him that, as he describes it, he uses the method of free association to become provocative in the context of some growing awareness of feeling connected with me over the weekend. This method of associating repeats his thoughts coming into the session where a good feeling is replaced by thoughts of an argument between us. The same process appears in the dream where being "in touch" leads to thoughts of a duel, and my becoming annoyed. There seemed to be something frightening about staying "in touch" with me. This led him to thoughts of how out of touch he felt, at times, with everyone and everything over the weekend. It takes on a whole new meaning now. This then led to some historical material that shed light on this issue.

In this example, the patient's use of the method of free association became an invitation to a duel as a defense against a feeling of greater closeness. It was the patient who was able to see that he was using the method of association as a way of keeping distant while attempting to establish even further distance via an invitation to the analyst to duel. Observing what he was doing with his associations became a powerful example of a method of relating that fit with his immediate experiences over the weekend, and with the dream. This was no hypothesized problem about working closely with me, but an example in the here and now of the session. This pattern of relating, that is, fighting in the face of loving feelings, was one of the issues that brought the patient into treatment as he was unable to form any stable love relationships. It has been my experience that if the analyst works closely and effectively with the patient's use of the method of free association, the act of associating itself becomes an intimate act involving the wish to touch and be touched. In a fully experienced treatment it becomes associated with an act of love, thus leading to numerous issues around it.

At certain phases of analysis the resistance will be expressed in the type of material the patient brings; at others it will revolve around the relationship of the patient to his or her own material.

A patient with a sadomasochistic character structure who usually fills the hour with recitations of how the world is treating her badly (and thereby invites the analyst to criticize her analytic performance), begins a session by telling of an incident in which she managed to extract herself from a potentially unpleasant situation at work. She then begins to relate a dream, and her associations lead her to divulge a heretofore unknown part of her history that throws new light on her character structure. The analyst makes a comment, and the patient returns to her usual way of talking, giving examples from life that show she is a victim.

Thus, it is at this point we see a change in the patient's "participating ego" that indicates there has been a change, often unconscious, in the patient's experience of the analytic process. The analyst is able to point to the observable moment where this change in voice has just happened to see what it was in the analyst's remark that led the patient to turn away from using the process to explore and learn more. Further, what is most crucial is the nature of the patient's experience that led her not to know or say how she was affected by the analyst's remark? This is the beginning of a resistance analysis, based on an observation of a change in the type of associations, which indicates the ego is participating in a different manner.

The concept of a *participating ego* helps us evaluate the patient's changes in voice with regard to his or her own thoughts.

A patient comes in complaining about how his corporate organization is infantilizing, and how he looks forward to the day when he can start his own business. He then gives various examples of the practices at work that seem to discourage independent functioning. As the patient talks, it is clear he sees the problems as primarily external. As he talks I am remembering the previous session, in which we had discovered his discomfort with an awareness of feelings of missing me when I was away for ten days. His sense was that he must be like some "little baby" if I can't go away for a while without his having a big reaction. He felt disgust with himself for having these feelings. As he continued to talk about work, he described how he couldn't wait to leave "here," at which point he paused, and then continued with his line of thought. I asked him if he had noted the pause after he said "here," and wondered if he had heard the ambiguity of where "here" was.

He acknowledged hearing it the same way, and I wondered what came to his mind about why he might not have been able to mention it at the time. He realized it was at odds with his awareness of his feelings about being in the session. He likes coming, but then he guessed that was just the point. Why couldn't he mention any of that? He described coming into my office today, and how inviting it seemed. The windows were open, and there was a warm breeze. It felt so good to be in here, but he guessed he felt he shouldn't enjoy it. I suggested these feelings seem to be associated today with being "infantile," for which he has some disgust. Thus, coming in today his thoughts go to a place that he is thinking of as "infantilizing," that he describes as wanting no part of. In response the patient's thoughts went to growing up, and how his family always did things together. He began this set of thoughts with what seemed like an explanation for how well cared for he was as a child. However, as he described the situation he became aware of a feeling of great sadness. It led him to remember that while everybody was always together, nobody was ever paid much attention to. While the feelings of sadness continued, heretofore unrelated examples of empathic failures on the part of both parents were brought to light. I suggested his longings to be cared for in a very individual way may not have been consistently met, leading him to believe there was something "infantile" about the feelings.

In this example there are two ways in which the concept of a participating ego helps us determine a resistance is in operation. The first is that the analysand is focusing on an external problem (i.e., the infantilizing corporation) without any expansion of his thought processes. Also, we can see a moment where the patient's ego seems to observe multiple meanings in "here," but then retreats from them. It is this moment, observable to both of us, that allows for the beginning discussion of the patient's resistance to the analytic process, the pleasure and comfort it brings him, and the feeling of threat associated with it. We then see a freeing up of the patient's thoughts. A more typical example of what may have been interpreted is the patient's initial discussion of the infantilizing corporation as really being about the patient's fears about the analysis. Not that this interpretation would be incorrect. However, it establishes the analyst as the knower of what is really going on, with the patient's associations as fodder for the analyst's understanding. This is in contrast to working with what is most observable to the patient, and inviting his or her ego to participate in the process. By keeping this key variable in mind we can determine certain resistances, and think of ways to talk with the patient about the process that don't bypass the ego's participation.

The concept of a participating ego, then, becomes one way of gauging the patient's involvement in the method of free association. Used as a guide, it helps evaluate the multiple resistances and actions the method can be put to (Holmes 1996). Yet, I cannot emphasize strongly enough that the method of working with resistances to individual content or the method of free association cannot be applied in a rigid manner. Once the analysand understands the significance of resistance analysis, it can be used for a variety of purposes. Thus, resistance interpretations can be induced by the patient and come to mean a criticism, attack, or intrusion, all with multiple meanings. *Therefore, the method needs to be applied with some degree of flexibility*.

Another axis along which the ego-psychological–influenced analyst may listen, as demonstrated in the above example, is patients' capacity to observe their own thoughts (i.e., observing ego). As noted throughout this monograph, this capacity (i.e., to observe one's own thoughts and see them as psychologically meaningful) is an important part of the change process that takes place in psychoanalysis. If it is being blunted, as when the patient notices the dual meaning of "here" and then retreats from it, interpreting as if an important resistance is not in operation may mean bypassing what is occurring within the ego. Interpreting underlying content, or even the resistance to certain content, while the ego is in the process of shunning observations, may lead one to bypass a crucial component in the capacity to change. We may get our patients to see another way of looking at the content via the seductiveness or forcefulness of our argument, but if we do not pay attention to the observing ego, we may ignore that part of the mind central to the development of a self-analytic process.

While I have presented the above discussion in a schematic fashion, the art of the method is in the details. Thus, the freedom to say what is on one's mind in analysis, and the capacity to observe one's own thoughts, is what develops over time in analysis. It is part of what analysis works toward. In the truly meaningful areas of patients' thoughts, they are incapable of freely saying or observing what is on their mind. It is part of what has brought them to treatment in the first place. Thus, the analyst listening for the role of the patient's participating or observing ego is a variable to be considered, not a demand to be met. The concepts of a participating and observing ego are offered as important variables in considering the ego's participation in the change process. They are not the only variables to be considered, nor are they always easy to judge or interpret. After a patient is in analysis for some time, the absence of an observing ego in a session may be an action, an ego regression, or part of the working-through process. The presence of an observing ego may represent the same phenomenon. However, without the concept of an ego doing something with the free association process, a valuable conceptual framework is lost.

Evaluations of patients' capacity to utilize their participating and observing ego are the specifics of what I have understood as the meaning of the term *therapeutic alliance*. This concept fell into disfavor (Brenner 1979, Friedman 1969) in part because of its initial presentation as a something akin to a consciously motivated direction of the analysis influenced by the relationship. However, as a touchstone for the intensity of resistance of the unconscious ego, the state of the therapeutic alliance can also be viewed as a "dynamic, integrated, and fluctuating component of the whole therapeutic process" (Novick and Novick 1996, p. 359).

To this point I have primarily emphasized the similarities between Paul Gray's work and my own. The areas of convergence are what set our work (along with others mentioned throughout the monograph as identified with contemporary ego psychology) apart from those writing about psychoanalytic technique from other perspectives. While Gray's work has been primarily in the area of ego psychology as seen through the lens of resistance analysis, there is a subtext throughout his work related to the ego's autonomous functions. It is this latter component I have focused on.

There are differences in our perspectives that I have written about previously (Busch 1995a) and that are demonstrated throughout this monograph:

1. The degree to which we need to rely on close process monitoring as the primary method of resistance analysis: I suggest that as analysis progresses, one expects greater autonomy and flexibility in ego functioning, leading to the possibility of interpreting resistances from a large-scale view of the patient's associations, potentially allowing for more complex observations on the resistances. For example, observing a patient suddenly shut down emerging feelings of sadness with a flip comment, we can follow where the associations go to see if information may be forthcoming on some component of the derivation of the resistance.

2. While Gray's view is that the primary threat to the ego in resistances is from a reexternalized superego, I see that threat as one among many, as varied and subtle as the nature of the resistances themselves. Theories of development from object relations and self psychology have been invaluable in identifying the variety of threats patients experience.

3. It has not been my impression that the capacity for self-observation develops spontaneously from resistance analysis, and that exploration of all sides of the conflict needs to take place to bring about expansion of the ego.

Other differences in our perspectives also exist. First, I tend to see resistances in terms of gradations rather than their being present or absent. It is another factor that leads me to a more flexible approach to changes in direction of the associations. For example, I would maintain that, at times, it is difficult to tell if a movement away from direct references to the analyst is a resistance to the transference or an association to the transference, or if the resistance is evidence (e.g., displacement) that there might still be usable information for the ego in the content. I tend to rely more on my general understanding of the patient and empathic attunement with what is occurring in the clinical moment than Gray, who finds these to be unreliable indicators. Therefore, although I believe I monitor the process closely, I do not use the method of close process monitoring to the degree to which Gray does.

Second, there are differences in our method of working with a resistance once it has been determined to be in operation. Once I point it out, increasingly I wait to see where patients' associations go to see which aspect of the resistance they are most able to explore at that time. The resistance itself is made up of many parts (e.g., the specific feeling of threat that brings it about; its adaptive component, both historic and current; the underlying contents). Patients choose which part to delve into, or to resist investigating, if that is what needs to be done at that point. Gray's method takes patients back to the time right before the resistance was expressed, and asks them to associate to the feeling that may have brought the resistance about. While this a more systematic approach, it may also be asking patients to bypass a resistance to this component of the resistance. Finally, as I have tried to demonstrate throughout this monograph, I have found myself interested in methods of engaging the patient's more autonomous ego functions other than resistance analysis. This revolves mainly around our methods of interpretation, which too frequently seem to bypass consideration of the ego. It is a different direction than the one taken by Gray, but inspired by his work.

In summary, this chapter discussed the scope of a contemporary ego-psychological approach. It is based on the premise that an important part of the change process in psychoanalysis revolves around modifications in the ego, and therefore it is in the best interest of the patient that the analyst take into account clinical methods that include the ego's participation. These methods focus on finding what Paniagua (1991) called the "working surface" in patients' use of the method of free association, while also utilizing their relationship to their own thoughts (i.e., participating and observing ego) as a guide to the state of the resistances. The goal of the treatment, in part, is expansion of the autonomous ego functions as demonstrated in increased capacity for thought and observation, as restricted ego functioning seems to be an important component of the fears and inhibitions that bring patients into treatment. These adaptations from an earlier time are kept in place, in part, because of the regressive nature of thoughts and feelings viewed through unconscious ego processes, which make fears seem more real and severely restrict the capacity to think differently about them.

4

A Brief History of Ego Psychology

Two of the most significant discoveries from the study of the ego, that is, the autonomy of the ego from the id and the unconscious ego resistances, have only begun to be integrated into what has been considered clinical psychoanalytic technique based on the structural model. How one views the significance of these discoveries has implications for psychoanalytic technique, in terms of both what one interprets and how one interprets. Our clinical modes at present, if they include the structural theory at all, generally stop with the ego and the id and the limitations of this model. Gray (1982, 1994) and I (Busch 1992, 1995a) have extensively covered how the significance of the unconscious ego resistances, based on Freud's (1926) second theory of anxiety, was never fully incorporated into Freud's clinical thinking, and has remained episodically integrated within the clinical technique of many analysts.

What is generally considered resistance analysis is not analysis of the *unconscious* ego resistances, which was one of the primary factors in Freud's moving toward the structural model. Further, when analyzing resistances, what is frequently misunderstood is that the threat is experienced and reacted to at an unconscious level. Thus what one is dealing with is an unconscious threat perceived by the unconscious ego. However, since the above line of thinking has been delved into at length elsewhere (Davison et al. 1990, Gray 1994, Pray 1994), I would like to focus here on a very brief history of the development of the ego concept, with special emphasis on the ego's autonomy from the id. We shall see that this is a concept that has not been integrated with clinical technique, in spite of the fact that its validity has been demonstrated many times. That is, the preponderance of data from sophisticated research on child development (Siegler 1991) shows that a variety of ego functions exist at birth or come into existence shortly thereafter, including primitive modes of thinking, perceiving, and ways of organizing the world. How much one considers those data an important variable in technique has much to do with how much one follows a model of including the ego as an equal co-partner in treatment. In contrast to this model, it has been my impression that many analyses are conducted as if the analysand spoke in tongues, with the analyst's role being one of a medieval mystic skilled in the art of translating secret languages.

It is not often enough mentioned that Freud saw his new theory in "The Ego and the Id" as not going "beyond the roughest outline" (1923, p. 12). It was a brilliant outline, but the tendency to stay stuck in certain elements of it while ignoring others has led to the growth of a clinical method that, at times, seems to reject crucial details of psychological functioning. Freud introduced the ego in this work as a coherent organization of mental processes with certain key functions. However, it is a critical point that the ego was still seen as a differentiated part of the id, and that its shape was seen as determined by the energies of the id. The ego is seen as the passive rider of the id horse, "obliged to ride it where it wants to go" (p. 25). It is this view of the ego that has dominated clinical technique in America and is the ego psychology we have been taught to practice. With his discussion of the second theory of anxièty Freud (1926) moves toward a more independent ego, but this is mainly in the area of the management of anxiety via defenses. The significance of unconscious resistances and their relationship to this second theory of anxiety was, as mentioned earlier, never fully integrated into clinical technique. By 1937 Freud had come to view the ego as having roots independent of the instincts, with its own innate, distinguishing characteristics. This change in his thinking was elaborated by some, but it is important to note that Arlow and Brenner's (1964) characterization of the ego as the *executant* of the id returns to a view of the ego dominated by the demands of the id. This change in perspective, which was in opposition to the growing view of a more autonomous ego, and colored Arlow and Brenner's clinical perspective, has, I believe, gone unnoticed.

From a theoretical perspective, our view of the ego was permanently changed by the work of Hartmann (1939, 1950, 1952), Hartmann and colleagues (1946), and Rapaport (1951, 1954, 1956, 1957). These authors presented the argument that man is not just at the mercy of drives, and that behavior is not guided only by unconscious motivation. In short, it was suggested that certain functions of the ego were inborn (e.g., apparatuses of perception, memory, and motility), and existed before the expression of conflict. Further, these primary or autonomous functions become the core of the ego, and in many cases remain outside the influence of the id. There are also ego functions that may have developed out of conflict, but that gain a certain independence from it and are thought of as secondary autonomous ego functions. In short, these authors postulated a constitution of the ego, which they believed warranted serious attention from psychoanalysts.

It was Rapaport's (1957) hope that once the theory of ego autonomy took hold as a useful conceptual tool, it would become a cornerstone of psychoanalytic technique. However, in this same paper he presciently recognized how far clinical technique lags behind theory, setting the stage for what existed almost four decades later (i.e., a theory of technique without a clear concept of ego). Intriguing ideas abound throughout the early theoretical papers on ego psychology. These papers are forerunners of recent attempts to introduce the ego back into clinical technique. For example, various comments by Rapaport touch on aspects of Gray's (1994) and my (Busch 1995a) work. Thus in his 1951 paper on the autonomy of the ego, Rapaport notes that the respect for the patient's ego autonomy is not simply a theoretical concept. He suggests that in certain cases it clearly marks the difference between therapeutic success and failure. Compare this with Gray's (1982) remark: "the therapeutic results of analytic treatment are lasting in proportion to the extent to which, during the analysis, the patient's unbypassed ego functions have become involved in a consciously and increasingly voluntary co-partnership with the analyst" (p. 624). Rapaport's (1954) injunction that, if one is considering the patient's ego as part of the process, interpretations cannot come out of the blue, is a forerunner of my earlier thinking:

> The patient must make some connection between what he is aware of thinking and saying, and the analyst's intervention. No matter how brilliant the analyst's reading of the uncon-

scious, it is not useful data until it can be connected to something the patient can be consciously aware of. [Busch 1993, p. 152]

Finally, Rapaport (1957) tells a story that captures the significance of the central role of the analysand's capacities for freedom of associations, and freedom of self-reflection as one important goal of the analytic process. It captures the significance of what seems like the crucial capacity for ongoing self-analysis as an antidote to the inevitability of enactments:

> A king returned to his capital followed by his victorious army. The band played and his horse, the army, the people, all moved in step with the rhythm. The king, amazed, contemplated the power of music. Suddenly he noticed a man who walked out of step and slowly fell behind. The king, deeply impressed, sent for the man, and told him: "I never saw a man as strong as you are. The music enthralled everybody except you. Where do you get the strength to resist it?" The man answered, "I was pondering, and that gave me the strength." [p. 724]

The question of why the discoveries of the greater role of the ego in development and psychic conflict did not lead to changes in technique is a complex one. Previously, Gray (1982) and I (Busch 1992) documented Freud's own ambivalence toward the structural model, while also suggesting that the sweeping explanatory power of unconscious fantasies has a seductive pull for all analysts. Hartmann's expansive view of the role of the ego in development, as part of a general psychology, may have paradoxically worked against its inclusion into clinical technique when considered alongside the absence of clinical data in Hartmann's work on the ego (Busch 1993). Further, it is often not stated, but Hartmann (1939) may have limited investigations into the role of the ego in psychoanalytic technique with this prediction: "It is probable that the study of this conflict-free ego sphere, though it is certainly not without technical significance (for instance, in the analysis of resistance), will in general contribute less to psychoanalytic technique than the study of conflict and defenses" (p. 9).

Rapaport (1956) clearly did not share Hartmann's views. However, his work on integrating the findings of ego psychology into clinical technique was mostly in the elucidation of types of thinking and feeling states of hospitalized patients, but it was never translated into specific clinical methodology with the ego at the center. While the effect of the work of Hartmann and Rapaport is obvious in such diverse areas as the ramification of early experience on the shape of the ego, the treatment of patients previously considered untreatable by psychoanalysis, and the elaboration of criteria for analyzability, just to name a few of the major alterations in our thinking in the last fifty years, their contributions to our understanding of the ego as part of our clinical technique have been far fewer. Clinical case conferences, whether for diagnostic or therapeutic purposes, still have as their main emphasis the unearthing of the central unconscious fantasy as the primary goal, with the analyst's role most often conceptualized in a similar manner.

The clinical application of Freud's new theory of the ego began with the work of Wilhelm Reich (1933), Anna Freud

(1936), Sterba (1934), Nina Searl (1936), and Fenichel (1941). In the midst of the Hartmann and Rapaport era, the most consistent work on the clinical application of the ego in psychoanalytic technique can be found in a series of papers written by Loewenstein (1950, 1952, 1953, 1962, 1966, 1971). While continuing to emphasize and add to our understanding of resistance analysis, Loewenstein was one of the first to articulate the recent discovery of the autonomous ego function for clinical technique. For example, in 1950 Loewenstein noted that since resistances are unconscious, "we must take into account that a very important part of the ego remains unconscious, so that an important part of the analyst's interpretations aim at bringing to consciousness unconscious ego phenomena" (p. 34). This is a point that, in my reading of the literature and in hearing clinical presentations, still seems not to be well integrated into our clinical understanding (Busch 1992, 1993). One can also find a harbinger of Gray's (1994) work on close process monitoring of resistances in the following Loewenstein (1962) observation:

> In other words, for the analysis it is as important to have the patient say what occurs to him as it is to observe how and why he is unable to do so. Not only does the analyst pay equal attention to the id, ego, and superego manifestations, but even the patient is expected to observe and express his emerging thoughts as well as his reluctance to perceive or verbalize them. [p. 178]

In 1952, Loewenstein articulated ways in which the discoveries of the ego impacted on technique. He described how, with the new ego psychology, the purpose of analysis changes from the recovery of memories to the reestablishment of connections via corrections of distortions brought about by the defense mechanisms. The psychoanalytic process changes from "bringing to consciousness" (p. 54) to "gaining of insight" (p. 54), once the synthetic and organizing functions of the autonomous ego are taken into consideration. This allows for the understanding of what happens to warded-off mental content and processes once they are available to the more conflict-free aspects of the ego. New solutions to pathogenic conflicts were now seen as the result of bringing the unconscious wishes and defenses to scrutiny by the autonomous ego (Loewenstein 1953). Finally, Loewenstein's (1966, 1971) emphasis on the analyst's reliance on the patient's autonomous ego functions to initiate and further the analytic process foreshadows Gray's (1982) observation on the results of treatment being predicated upon the degree to which the patient's ego functions are not bypassed as part of the process.

However, several insufficiencies in explanation may have played a role in what happened to the general thrust of Loewenstein's pioneering work. That is, Loewenstein's contributions are generally unrecognized in the current literature, and his emphasis on the role of the ego in clinical technique became subtly undermined by a slight but significant change in emphasis, resulting in the understanding of the role of the ego, at best, to go no further in development than where Loewenstein left it. Thus, Loewenstein's understanding of resistance analysis had, within it, certain limitations. For example, he began (1950) by viewing resistances as against the instincts rather than feelings of threat or danger generated in the ego as described in Freud's (1926) second theory of anxiety (Busch 1992). He saw this latter point as a special case necessitating what he called "reconstruction upward" (p. 36). However, this was just the point of Freud's second theory of anxiety. Unless one is clear as to the nature of the patient's experience of resistances, the analyst is interpreting in the wrong direction. Without a clear understanding that one is dealing with unconscious fears and senses of danger or threat, the whole question of how resistance analysis works, and what causes it to work, gets murky.

Analyzing the unconscious feelings of threat and danger leads to patients' greater freedom to think, feel, and understand areas that were previously unknowable to them. Without this basic concept, Loewenstein (1962, 1971) is forced to rely on the importance of the relationship with the analyst, as Freud did and as many current theorists do, in order to overcome resistances. If one does not understand the dynamics of analyzing resistance and its role in the patient's feeling of safety, one is forced to invoke the importance of the relationship in dealing with resistance. To see the relationship as the main factor in dealing with resistances is the difference between overcoming and analyzing resistances. Further, even though Loewenstein (1952) was one of the first to highlight the importance of exposing conflicts to the synthetic and organizing function of the ego, his explanations for why this was important left much to be desired.

Explanations from studies into the developmental steps in cognitive functioning, as, for example, in the work of Piaget

(1930, Piaget and Inhelder 1959), although supporting Loewenstein's position, were not yet available to psychoanalysts at the time. Thus, understanding that a patient, in his or her area of conflict, is characteristically thinking at a regressed level in some very specific but subtle ways, helps explain why exposing these methods of thinking and the reasons for them to the light of what Loewald (1971) called higher level ego functioning can be part of the curative process, and crucial for the increased mastery of a conflict area. Without such a process occurring, the patient's thinking in conflict areas remains much closer to actions, thus making it far more difficult to gain some modicum of mastery over these conflicts in action (Busch 1995b). Thus, although Loewenstein made enormous contributions to the development of analytic technique with the ego at the center, he was limited by the understanding of the time. Insufficiencies in the model were not well understood, and the significant changes made by theorists who followed were included under the umbrella of Loewenstein's approach, while the actual thrust of their work could be quite different.

5

Object Relations and the Structural Model

At various times classical technique has been cast by the relationalists, interpersonalists, self psychologists, and intersubjectivists as an instinctually based, non–object-related theory of pathology and technique. While this position is not without truth, it is important to have a sense of the history of this perspective. By 1914 one sees evidence of Freud struggling with the role of object relations in the formation of symptoms in particular, and human behavior in general. As is often the case with Freud, he saw this foray as a beginning exploration and not the final word. As noted by Sandler and colleagues (1991) in their discussion of "On Narcissism,"

> the essay may justly be considered as one of a series of turning points in Freud's thinking, opening up our understanding of motivation as stemming from something other than instinctual gratification, and presaging not only structural theory but object-relations theory, as well as the importance of the self concept as opposed to the ego, and many other subsequent theoretical developments. Freud, as he makes clear in his text, was well aware that he was initiating a long-running discussion, not preempting a topic—for example, when he lists a number of specific "themes which I propose to leave on one side, as an important field of work which still awaits exploration" [p. 92]. We are safe in assuming that Freud called his essay on narcissism "An Introduction" deliberately; he was being prescient, not coy. [pp. ix–x]

However, Freud's views are presented in a language and conceptual framework heavily weighted down by an energy model. The result is confusing in that while we know we are glimpsing Freud's new insights, these are blunted by his attempts to reduce these findings to a now archaic tension-reduction model. For example, in likening hypochondriachal symptoms to genital excitement, he notes that any part of the body can be substituted for the genitals.

> We can decide to regard erotogenicity as a general characteristic of all organs and may then speak of an increase or decrease of it in a particular part of the body. For every change in the erotogenicity of the organs there might then be a parallel change of libidinal cathexis in the ego. Such factors would constitute what we believe to underlie hypochondria and what may have the same effect upon the distribution of libido as is produced by a material illness of the organs. [Freud 1914b, p. 84]

Yet, as Yorke (1991) notes, despite Freud's attempts to remain within an economic, libidinal framework, his psychological insights propel themselves into this essay. Thus, after a long discourse on the role of cathectic distribution (i.e., overabundance of ego cathexis in contrast to object cathexis) in hypochondriasis, the following can be taken as a summation of the topic based on an energy model, or Freud's romantic vision of the human heart: "A strong egoism is a protection against falling ill, but in the last resort we must begin to love in order not to fall ill, and we are bound to fall ill if, in consequence of frustration, we are unable to love" (p. 85).

The different interpretations of this passage have been characterized by Holt (1972) as representing Freud's mechanistic and humanistic view of man. These two perspectives represent the fulcrum of the psychoanalytic dialectic over the past eighty years. The result has been the development of two brands of psychoanalysis: one embraces the significance of the object in psychological functioning but rejects Freud's models of the mind, and the other accepts Freud's models of the mind but has tended to reject the significance of the object in psychological functioning. Most germane to the topic at hand, the ego in the structural theory of technique, we seem to have ended up with object relations and self-psychological theories without an ego, and a structural theory without objects.

An object-relations perspective was part of ego psychology from its inception, beginning with Hartmann's (1939) views on adaptation, which was a major impetus for research into the effects of early object relations on the development of the child. From another perspective Hartmann and Kris (1945) wrote,

> The object of psychoanalytic observation is according to Freud not the individual in splendid isolation; it is part of a world. Psychoanalysis does not claim to explain human behavior only as a result of drives and fantasies; human behavior is directed toward a world of men and things. [p. 25]

Rapaport (1956) states,

> Clinically these considerations may be illustrated by the well-known fact that a patient's picture of his environment as hostile and persecutory need not be entirely—and may not be at all—a projection. His environment may actually be what he describes it to be, and indeed may have come about in part as a matter of "social compliance" to the patient who "provoked" this. [p. 611]

The contemporary nature of these statements is noteworthy, and predates by some thirty years the current contemplations of the psychoanalytic situation as a joint production of patient and analyst. However, the structural theory has come to be seen as antithetical to an object relations perspective in general and to any consideration of analysis as, at times, a two-party construction. How has this come about? It is my view that the prevalent interpretation of the structural model has eschewed the significance of object relations as part of symptom formation and technique. What was integrated by the structuralists of the 1950s was replaced by a return to a model of conflict and treatment that was based on the reemergence of the heightened significance of the role of the instinctual derivatives. The significance of what Schafer (1985) called a "developmental-environmental-functional" (p. 543) approach was viewed as an ancillary factor in understanding of pathology. Viewing these matters as ancillary is not an inherent part of the structural model, but it has come to be taken as such. It has been left to other theories to explore the significance of object relationships ignored by many contemporary structuralists. It has left the structuralists as easy targets, with other theories often establishing therapeutic models, it seems, primarily in opposition to this perspective.

Arlow's (1985) paper on the preeminent role of unconscious fantasies in psychic life captures the paradox inherent in attempting to build a treatment model without consideration of the role of object relations on development. In this paper, while championing the role of unconscious fantasies in intrapsychic conflict, he disavows the significance of so-called real events for pathology. Yet, at the same time, he demonstrates the importance of real events in his clinical thinking. What we see, in fact, is Arlow accepting and using certain realities of past object relations in his understanding of the patient, while denying the significance of a particular perception of an event that hardly seems crucial to the main issue. Arlow presents the following case:

A man is rebuked by his daughter after he criticized her for not informing her husband that she would be home late one evening. The patient feels protective of his son-in-law, and when his daughter became angry, anxiety developed around his belief that she wouldn't want to see him again. As background data, the patient had a one-year-older adopted brother who was very aggressive, and had severe learning problems. When the patient was 5, his adopted brother was placed in a home for retarded and disturbed children. He was never able to visit his brother, nor was the brother ever mentioned again in the family.

In describing the effects of these events on his patient, Arlow highlights the patient's relief at no longer being attacked by his brother, his belief that his wishes sent his brother away, and his overwhelming sense of guilt. He began to believe an injustice had been done to his brother, already an outsider, and he now wanted him back. He wanted to protest to his mother, but he saw what she did to children who were bad. He developed anxiety attacks when his mother would leave for the day.

In making a case for the significance of distorted elaborations of reality in unconscious fantasies, Arlow (1985) unnecessarily needs to place the significance of important object relations in opposing terms. Thus he states,

> If we could avail ourselves of the services of the proverbial "fly on the wall," that is, the unseen, nonparticipatory observer, who could furnish us with a complete and objective record of what happened, how useful would it be for the psychoanalytic enterprise? Not very, I suspect. What we deal with is how our patients have integrated their experiences and the nature and intensity of the persistent conflicts generated. [p. 529]

To make a point Arlow sets up an adversarial relationship between the use of reality (or versions of it) in the establishment of unconscious fantasies, and the importance of key object relationships in our patient's psychic life. Would Arlow suggest that this patient's having an aggressively out-of-control adopted brother, who was sent away and never spoken of again, had no effect upon him? Would he expect the same psychic constellation if his brother had been an easygoing child who had stayed at home? Arlow's own thinking would suggest not:

> He realized he had misperceived his daughter in terms of his mother. His son-in-law was the adopted outsider, a representative of the brother. The patient had acted out his childhood fantasy. He had defended his brother/son-in-law, and for his efforts, he had been scolded. Now he could only anticipate abandonment and ostracism. [p. 528]

In short, there seems to be no doubt about the profound effect of the fact that the patient had an aggressive, acting-out, adopted brother who was abandoned by his family. How could it be otherwise? This is not to say that one can predict the effect of such events beforehand. Certainly one needs to keep in mind the potentially distorting effect of wishes and conflicts that results in the specifics of how an event comes to be characterized. However, to disregard the significance of object relations is to simplify the contributing factors to psychic life. While championing the effects of unconscious fantasy on psychic life, Arlow de-emphasizes the role of reality events in these fantasies, as well as the distorting effects on the ego of certain developmental interferences. As noted earlier in this monograph, would we doubt for a moment that an actual seduction of a child would likely have a far different effect on the psychic structure than a fantasized seduction? This was the thrust of Rapaport's and Hartmann's contributions to ego psychology, but it has not been fully integrated within the perspective of those most identified with the structural model.

As noted earlier, when Arlow (1985) brings up a situation where a bee flies into his consulting room and describes the variety of reactions patients might have as primarily dependent on the strength of feminine, passive wishes, he leaves out many other possibilities, such as the different abilities of analysands' egos to maintain distance from an unconscious fantasy based on, for example, actual trauma. The earlier the trauma, the greater the difficulty a patient is likely to have in distinguishing fantasy from reality, especially in the areas of conflicts that develop around the trauma. The difference in a patient's ego capacity to gain some distance from feeling intruded upon may be based, in part, on how much the patient's bodily integrity has been violated by such things as surgical or other intrusive medical procedures, enemas, or ongoing patterns of disregard for the child's autonomy. In a little-known article, Sachs (1967) describes a case where a real event was treated as a fantasy, and only upon reanalysis were the patient and analyst able to understand the devastating effects on the ego (e.g., obsessional doubting, difficulty in distinguishing reality from fantasy) of the parental coercion to deny the event, and the re-traumatization via enforcement of the denial in the first analysis by treating it as a fantasy.

Pine's (1988) emphasis on the need to keep in mind various explanatory theories has always struck me as an ideal perspective for the analyst. There are many underlying causes of behavior, and the more routes of understanding we can help our patients to gain, the more effective will be their own attempts to understand the inevitable postanalytic regressions that occur. For example, by ruling out an object relations perspective and the effects such experiences have on various aspects of the psychic structure, we deprive our patients of understanding one of the many factors that may have led to their current dilemma. Further, it does more harm than good in cases of remembered mistreatment by nonpsychotic patients to describe their experiences as being due to a feeling or memory of being mistreated. By describing patients' experiences in this manner, we undermine one of our most important allies in the analytic process—patients' autonomous ego functions. It is as if we are saying to the patient, without explanation, "You may think such and such has happened, but we will see about the truth value of this experience, and I will be the final determiner of truth here." It is an explicit challenge to the patient's ego and will be experienced by him or her in this way. In this manner we are repeating what is a familiar reenactment in many families—the denial of pathology and the undermining of the patient's ego.

On the other hand, I am not suggesting that we take the truth of analysands' depictions of others at face value. In the majority of cases it is the meaning of such depictions in the context of the rest of the patients' associations that is the main issue at hand. However, it is a disservice to patients if one of the meanings of their associations, that is, the ways they were or are dealt with by others, is considered less significant than their unconscious fantasy of these same objects. While it would not surprise us to discover patients' mistreatment of those whom they accuse of mistreatment, or evidence of provocation of those experienced as victimizers, these dynamics are another piece of the puzzle that is primarily understandable to the patient in the context of current associations and/or observable transferences. It certainly does not negate the patient's perception of being mistreated, and more likely than not is the result of it. We are always dealing with some approximation of the truth, and never with ultimate truths. Yet we have acted as if to validate one set of truths is to invalidate others. This has been especially the case with regard to the role of past and present object relations among those who have seen themselves as upholding the tenets of the structural model.

In a similar vein, Arlow's view that the analyst's feelings serve primarily as a kind of day residue to unconscious fantasies in the transference has hampered investigation of the analyst's role in the formation of the transference, and has made it seem like there is no room for such a perspective within the structural model. The same can be said for Brenner's (1976) suggestion that if the analyst is on the right track, almost any interpretation he or she makes will be helpful. There are many ways to make an intervention, and some may be more helpful than others. Suffice it to say at this point that we have been left with an erroneous perception that there is little room for an object relations perspective within the structural view of the transference.

Abend's (1982) reflections on the analytic implications of self-disclosure suggest some of the difficulties that have become associated with a view of the structural model. While his actual presentation is in the form of an extended question, and his conclusions are presented as a caveat rather than a statement of fact, I will discuss the sentiments to which I believe others have been led rather than what was intended by Abend. Abend's stance on self-disclosure revolves around his belief that on the one hand, too much factual information may inhibit the range of expression of patients' reactions, and on the other, all reality information will be "understood primarily in terms of its unconscious ramifications for the patient" (p. 376). He also raises a crucial observation that self-disclosure may serve unconscious purposes for the analyst. It is a point often overlooked in the literature on self-disclosure. Thus, just because we believe we are being nonauthoritarian, or helpful, or open, it does not mean it will be perceived this way by the patient, and it should not preclude consideration of the unconscious motives of the analyst in his or her actions. Yet, what has become clearer from the work of those associated with the relational, interpersonal, and social constructionist schools is that there are unconscious motivations and gratifications in everything we do in the treatment. What, when, and how we interpret are all subject to influence from unconscious motivations. This does not mean we don't make interpretations because it might lead to an unconscious gratification for the analyst. By attempting to minimize the analyst's burdening the patient with his or her unconscious gratifications, we may well burden our patients in other ways.

Abend (1982) reports taking an unusual break in his work with patients because of his serious medical condition. The time of his return was left unspecified, and there was no accompanying explanation. In this situation a very unusual event is occurring that will deeply affect the patient. Yet patients were asked to treat it as something that was only going on in their minds. If the electricity in the analyst's office suddenly went out, would we expect the analyst and patient to act like nothing unusual was happening? Such a position does not take into account that in extraordinary situations like this the patient might have some legitimate reality concerns about his or her analysis and the analyst's capacity to continue analyzing. The significance of the analyst for the analysis and the analysand is being discounted. It is akin to a patient who, in response to an extended break in the treatment, can only allow herself to think of separations in the distant past. Thus, to spare his patients the burden of unconscious gratification in his disclosure, Abend may have burdened his patients by placing them in an infantilized position in which they were asked to set aside certain ego functions (e.g., perception, self-protection, and survival).

Upon returning to his practice with visible signs of his recent surgery, Abend finds himself unable to keep to the position of nondisclosure that he believes to be technically most correct. He raises the possibility that disclosure in this situation is likely a countertransference, rather than an indication of his basic humanity that allows for the work of analysis to continue. In the one example Abend presents, his disclosure leads to an outpouring of feelings on the part of the patient and useful analytic work. Abend considers the possibility that his not needing to hide his condition under these extraordinary considerations may have helped the patient feel more open to her own feelings of anger and guilt. However, he is more impressed with how information gets processed within the context of unconscious dynamics. His conclusion is subtly judicious, and one most analysts can agree with—that even if it is in the best interest of the analysis to share factual information, it still serves unconscious purposes for the analyst that are important to pay attention to. While no doubt true, it leaves out certain variables that are a necessary component of any analysis for creation of an atmosphere of honest, if sometimes painful, self-revelation.

While there is a lot to be learned in this area, when it comes to obvious influences the analyst's actions are having on the analysis, I agree with Renik's (1995b) perception: "Whereas an analyst's effort to be anonymous is supposed to allow the patient greater freedom to associate, the opposite is the case in my experience" (p. 483). Recent excesses in the trend toward self-disclosure seem a reaction to excesses in the other direction. In my experience lack of self-disclosure may place as great a burden on patients as too much disclosure. We demand restrictions in ego functions of the patient by not disclosing.

The analyst as blank screen became the idealized method for those associated with the structural model. However, as I have viewed the structural model, it is the analysand's capacity to freely experience, know, and reflect upon his or her thoughts that is of prime importance in the analytic process. This model encourages freedom of thought, which becomes a guiding light for the analyst's behavior, and as I have indicated elsewhere (Busch 1995c) there are many ways the analyst approaches the analytic process that encourages increasing independence of thought, or passivity and dependence on the analyst. Too little factual information can have just as much of an inhibiting effect on the patient's freedom to think as too much information. To take just one example, it has been my experience that if we convey to patients that there is something unusual going on, but we make it seem as if it is nothing, it has a greater inhibitory effect on thinking than acknowledging that something is going on.

In summary, Freud initiated efforts to understand the role of object relations in development, and it seemed to be an integral part of the thinking of the early ego psychologists. Yet, this perspective has remained peripheral to interpretations of the structural model over the last thirty years, both in and out of analysis. Arlow (1985) diminishes the object relations perspective by pointing to how useless it would be for the analyst to know what "really happened" (the analyst as fly-on-the-wall). However, as noted earlier, Arlow contradicts this argument by demonstrating the myriad ways he takes into account object relations in his clinical thinking. The eschewal of an object relations perspective as part of the structural model has had the unfortunate effect of leading those theorists who have taken up the banner of an object relations perspective to throw out the proverbial baby, and a number of bathroom fixtures, with the bathwater.

6

The Schools of
Object Relations

The landscape of psychoanalytic thoughts has dramatically changed with the infusion of insights from theoretical schools that highlight the role of relationships (e.g., internal, external, projected, selfobject, analytic, etc.) in the formation and amelioration of psychic conflict. These schools include the relational, social constructivist, interpersonal, intersubjective, object relations, and self-psychological perspectives (see Aron [1996] for a succinct summary of these perspectives). Their insights have enriched our knowledge and added another dimension of subtlety to our understanding of the effects of significant relationships on human development, the complex ways in which these are integrated and translated into human behavior, and how these relationships, especially the analytic relationship, may affect the tone and shape of all analyses.

Many analysts' working models include the following possible explanations for why a patient feels that the analyst's interpretation means the analyst has badly misunderstood something:

1. a momentary lapse in the analyst's empathy leading to the patient's feeling excessively narcissistically injured due to early faulty mirroring;
2. the patient's intolerance of the analyst's freedom to think his or her own thoughts, based on an identification with a narcissistically demanding, controlling parent;
3. the analyst's unconscious identification with an absent or hurtful parent;
4. the patient's extreme discomfort with the analyst's growing importance to him or her, related to an unconscious

twin fantasy (e.g., "We are supposed to feel exactly the same"; "I am not supposed to have to long for you");

5. the analyst's unconscious need to assert his or her individuality in response to feeling marginalized, deadened, or discarded by a patient unconsciously identified with the aggressor, and who hears his rage coming back at him in the analyst's comments;

6. the analyst's remarks as a repetition of a trauma revolving around an interference with the patient's wishes to roam free in his or her own thoughts as an expression of a newfound freedom to explore.

These formulations, coming from different object relations perspectives, demonstrate the variegated psychological landscape the object relations perspective offers the psychoanalytic clinician. Mitchell (1988, 1993, Greenberg and Mitchell 1983), a leading proponent of the relational perspective and one of its most articulate spokespersons, has recently presented a beautifully rendered clinical description that captures the breadth of understanding offered by an object relations perspective to an ego-psychological model:

> Although Angela's sadomasochistic fantasies were sexual in content, from an ego psychology perspective they reflect a more fundamental and formidable psychological dilemma. From this perspective, she was not sneaking forbidden oedipal gratification by disguising it as pain. Rather, she was struggling with how she might satisfy her need for human contact and pleasure when it led to a terrifying sense of psychic dissolution, trying to construct a barrier against the threat of disintegrating merger when the very act of pushing away

required her calling on aggressive forces within herself that seemed murderous in potential. Her sadomasochistic masturbatory fantasy offered a kind of makeshift yet creative structure in the face of this dilemma, allowing and regulating needed contact with others, while simultaneously expressing and containing her aggression. [Mitchell and Black 1995, p. 56]

This is an example of how an ego-psychological and object relations perspective can be combined in a manner that allows for rich, complex understanding of fantasies that seem inherently abusive, but that actually serve as a connection to people in a way that is self-protective. In response to a threat of dissolution in the face of closeness, an enduring model of sadomasochistic relationships is established as a means of maintaining an object tie. It is a complex, creative act of the ego that leads to a defense against a threat in a way that both meets certain basic needs and avoids the threat.

I believe, along with Pine (1988), that the analyst needs to approach the clinical material with many models in order to comprehend, as deeply as possible, the range of feelings and fantasies fueling conflict. With this in mind, I will present some examples of how I use understanding derived from the schools of object relations within an ego-psychological perspective. I will start with a blending of the ego- and self-psychological models.

Mr. D., a successful entrepreneur who frequently felt unappreciated, was giving a public lecture on opportunities in his field. While part of him wanted me, his analyst, to attend this lecture, it was also clear that he didn't want me to attend, and he was afraid he couldn't stop me. In our session the day of the lecture he was uncharacteristically vague and distracted. He reported feeling well prepared, and looking forward to the presentation. However, this was said in a halting, distracted manner, which he noted, and his thoughts continued in this vein. He then remarked on how vague his thoughts were, and this was followed by associations to a series of incidents where he was feeling irritated with someone who was not attuned to his needs, and he then turned these feelings of irritation on himself. For example, he described having a meeting with a senior colleague to discuss a joint business venture. The colleague kept returning the discussion to some previous business deal he had done with great success. Mr. D. followed this with a variety of self-denigrating thoughts regarding his ungratefulness for not being willing to listen to this man.

After hearing this same sequence in various forms, I pointed out how he had noted earlier that he was vague in his thinking regarding his lecture. He then presented various situations where he was irritated with someone who was more attuned to his own needs rather than to Mr. D.'s but he then seemed to become uncomfortable with this feeling and turned it on himself. Since his association to his vagueness in the session was with feeling irritated with someone who he felt was not attuned to his needs, I wondered if his vagueness had to do with his discomfort with feelings of annoyance with me.

Mr. D. then remembered having a thought in the waiting room immediately before our appointment. He could not understand where it came from, and it immediately disappeared until I brought up that he might be having some feeling toward me. He imagined saying to me, upon my entering the waiting room, "You are a cretin." He then remembered a time in elementary school when he had said this to his father. This occurred after a fellow student had said this about his father, making Mr. D. extremely uncomfortable about his father's plan to coach his Little League baseball team. By saying this to his father, he hoped his father would get the message that he shouldn't coach and subject his son to the expected ridicule from other kids. Within this mind-set he was surprised when both his parents got angry at his remark. He didn't feel it had to do with how he really felt about his father, but at the moment had more to do with his fragile self-esteem. He loved his father, and felt terrible over what an ingrate he was for making the remark.

I suggested to the patient that we might now understand his vagueness when beginning the session as a response to a thought he would like to have kept vague. The thought was of saying something to me that might lead me to be angry with him. However, he was afraid I would misconstrue his meaning, not understanding that it had more to do with how he felt about himself. He then remembered thinking earlier that he was afraid someone at the lecture would know me, and figure out I was his analyst. He didn't want anyone to know of his analysis, because it was private. He had imagined telling me not to come to his lecture, but feared I would be offended.

In this example, a basic ego-psychological perspective on resistance analysis fits nicely with a self-psychological understanding of what is causing the sense of threat. It is a demonstration of how self psychology has enriched our understanding of a developmental line regarding the solidity or fragility of the sense of self. It has given us a more finely textured view of the potential threats experienced by the ego that lead to inhibitions in functioning. The particular resistance, seen in the patient's vagueness as a response to discomfort around keeping a thought out of his mind, seemed to be the result of his wish to bolster his fragile sense of well-being, and his feeling this would be interpreted as hostile. While the unconscious hostility and the invitation to a sadistic attack in Mr. D.'s statement were obvious, what he could most easily be aware of at this time was his guilt over the wish to protect his sense of self-worth. It was the uneasiness over the wish to protect himself that was most easily demonstrated in his associations. It is with this layer of understanding that the self psychologists have been most helpful. Most of the disturbances of the self and their consequences fit well within this ego-psychological method.

To this point I have discussed the manner in which an object relations perspective helps one's understanding of particular dynamics. However, there are also ways of thinking about issues of clinical technique that have come from those identified with these perspectives that have also enriched our understanding. One of the most striking has to do with the analyst's impact on the analytic situation (Hoffman 1983, 1987, 1992). Here is an example of how this perspective has informed my own clinical work, helping me to explore issues with greater confidence.

The patient, a third-year medical student, had been asked to take a leave of absence after his first year of classes because of poor grades. After a year of analysis he felt comfortable enough to return to school, and had done well. He had always thought he would go into medical research or pathology, but had recently done a psychiatry rotation and had become excited by it. He had thoughts about doing a psychiatry residency and becoming a psychoanalyst.

He began the session by noting how many thoughts he has from the time I greet him in the waiting room to the time he lies on the couch, and how infrequently he comments on them. He realizes he has this system where he rigidly believes treatment begins when he lies on the couch, and that these other thoughts he discards as silly. It is dawning on him that he is concerned about bringing up certain thoughts.

For example, he realized today that he was having thoughts he didn't want to mention. Specifically, when he came into the driveway this morning, some bushes were overgrown, preventing him from easily parking in the patient's parking space. He then tried to park there anyway, but ended up having to get out of his car awkwardly and duck the bushes. He then wondered why he was going on about this. In the past when he told me about this, I arranged to have the bushes trimmed, and there was no further problem. What was the big deal?

I suggested to him that he seemed to have some uneasiness with these thoughts. First he found himself reluctant to report them. Then, shortly after talking about this thought that some "Busch" didn't leave him enough room to park, he broke off this line of thought.

He found himself thinking about his clerkship in internal medicine. The chief resident had been very friendly to the medical students when they first began. He was interested in them, and concerned about it being a meaningful experience for them. The patient continued, "There was one guy in the group who was really sharp. He was planning to go into internal medicine, and he got very involved in the clerkship. It was clear he had a knack for thinking about clinical issues in a way the rest of us couldn't match. As time went on, the chief resident seemed to be a little hard on this guy. With the rest of us he remained the same, but there was this subtle difference with this other guy. It was like he was threatened by this guy's expertise." "Like there wouldn't be room for this guy in internal medicine?" I said. (Brief pause.) "Oh, I get it. Like there wasn't room for me in the driveway. But how would it apply here?"

I said, "I wonder if it isn't related to your expressing some thoughts recently about becoming a psychoanalyst."

The patient responded, "Hmm. It makes me think of my father. How I always felt there wasn't enough room for both of us in conversations. He would always have to make his point."

While we had talked about this aspect of his relationship with his father before, I wondered if he might be talking about him, somebody from the past, because there is something uncomfortable about talking about the present, such as his thoughts that there is a way I may be that may lead him to feel there isn't room for him in my area—psychoanalysis. He responded, "We must be on to something because I'm feeling really uncomfortable. I find myself wanting to be reassuring and say, 'No, it can't possibly be something about you. It must be my father or something.' But the evidence seems pretty clear. I'm uncomfortable."

A major advance in clinical technique has come from those who remind us of the analyst's contribution to the ambiance of the analysis, whether in the form of the analyst's unique personality or unanalyzed character traits, or as an enactment of a counterpart to an ongoing transference. In the context of a multifactorial understanding of behavior, it is another component of an in-depth exploration of determinants. In the example above, the patient begins the session with a thought that previously was dismissed, that is, that the thoughts he had before getting on the couch are relevant to the analysis. A shift has occurred that allows him to bring these thoughts to awareness. It suggests that there has been a shift in the "workable surface," an expansion of the ego's ability to be aware of something new. My understanding of the specific thoughts he is bringing to awareness has to do with his feeling that I am preventing him from doing something. He then backs away from this thought, and we have a resistance in action.

As I bring the resistance to his attention, I have an inkling there is something awry in my response, a "Busch" preventing him from parking in his space. I am uneasy about something in my response, but I can't quite capture it at the moment. What I can see now is that I may have bypassed an opportunity to explore the feeling that led to the resistance, and instead alluded to the underlying content. Further, in exploring the content, I went further than I might ordinarily have gone. My remark appears exhibitionistic to me, in that I am more interested in showing what I can see than checking what the patient can hear. In such a situation, where I am not sure that the patient has heard the reference to me, I would most often explore this aspect first. The patient may be more vague about the specifics of his associations for defensive purposes, and this needs to be taken into account. It is a subtle but important difference in approaching a resistance.

Ordinarily, after pointing out the movement away from the thoughts, I might ask the patient if he was aware of the link between the offending plant and my name. If he wasn't aware of it, I would proceed more cautiously than if he was able to be conscious of it and then withheld the thought. In the latter instance I might explore this aspect first. I frequently try to find the workable surface. In my remark to the patient I was not following my usual method of working. This in itself can have multiple meanings, but can only be understood in the context of the patient's associations and self-exploration.

The patient's associations here go to the interaction of the chief resident and the medical student. It is presented as a displacement, once removed from the transference. Once again, we can see how I bypass the defensive aspects. The patient's need to keep the thought in displacement is not acknowledged. Again, I was having an inkling that I was going further with these remarks than was warranted with this patient at this time. The patient's affect in going to the transference—"This must have to do with my father"—was desultory, and a sign that the association may be a defense against something specific he was feeling or seeing in the relationship. Here, also, I found myself picking up on a defense more quickly than I might ordinarily have done. I was reacting more to intuitive feelings, which I believe, in general, need to be filtered in the context of the patient's associations. I was being clever rather than empathic. It is one of those moments Renik (1993) describes when the analyst learns about his thinking via his actions. Although overdetermined, it became clearer at a later time that my response came, in part, from a growing unconscious feeling that there was little room for me in the patient's mind other than as a generic analyst or transference figure (e.g., "I must be confusing you with . . ."). The hidden message in this was that I was not worth considering. My mistakes, my motivations, my personality were being dismissed in a defensive identification with two self-absorbed parents. I became more aware of my need to find space for myself in the sessions, and the contribution of unacknowledged feelings of competition, resulting in my not leaving enough space for the patient at times. Other currents were also enacted. While consciously thinking that the patient would make a good psychoanalyst, I later realized I was reacting to the hostile aspects of his wishes (i.e., the bushes would need to be cut back so that he could have his space). It was an understandable part of the patient's dynamics, given that his father was neither welcoming nor facilitative of his entry into manhood, and clearly touched off certain personal issues for me. What was noteworthy was my need to enact this before understanding it. Also interesting is that with another patient in the throes of a good-enough working alliance the same methods may not have been an enactment.

However, there are also important differences in the models of pathology and in the models of technique of the ego-psychological and object relations schools, and these need to be highlighted if meaningful investigation and discussion is to take place. (In this chapter I focus primarily on the relational school, although much of what I say is applicable to the other schools of object relations.) The overarching difference revolves around the centrality of the relational world in the formation and amelioration of symptoms. Are there irreconcilable differences or, as Aron (1996) suggested, has the relational perspective tended to eschew the one-person psychology as a necessary corrective to the overemphasis placed on this view in classical psychoanalysis? Only continued mutual exploration of our differences will help determine their significance for clinical technique. There are some basic paradigms that separate the perspectives:

1. In the relational model conflict is a "relational configuration" (Mitchell 1988, p. 10). Neurotic symptoms are the result of "conflictual relational configurations unable to be syntonically woven into the dominant themes within the composition of the personality and finding circuitous, displaced disguised forms of expression" (p. 277). Patients' internal world of object relations is of prime significance, but not their intrapsychic world and

not intrapsychic conflict. Structures of the mind, such as the ego, and their role in mediating between conflicting goals, functions, or internal representations to safeguard a sense of safety are not a part of the relational model of the mind. Especially in the past, hostility toward an ego-psychological perspective was rampant.

> An inevitable consequence of this view is the so-called "analysis of resistance" so common in current practice which, at best, is a waste of time and, at worst, encourages the analysand to reform his ego into something that is presumably modeled on the aspirations of the analyst himself. [Thompson 1985, as quoted in Spezzano 1993, p. 209]

2. As a corollary to the above, Mitchell's (1988) significant paradigm shift is that now "mind has been defined from a set of predetermined structures emerging from inside an individual organism to transactional patterns and internal structures derived from an interactive, interpersonal field" (p. 17). In contrast, the ego-psychological perspective holds that mind includes a set of deep structures that forms along developmental lines in interaction with the drives, the inter- and intrapersonal field, other structures within the mind, and predetermined capacities, among a multitude of other factors. I would agree with Jacobs (1997), who states,

> In the excitement and enthusiasm for the new and creative possibilities inherent in the idea that two individuals, two minds, two histories, and two lives are

joined in the analytic enterprise and that learns from and affects the other, it is good to remember that psychoanalysis is also a one-person psychology in that *its ultimate goal is the exploration and understanding of the mind of the patient and that all that we learn about ourselves in the course of our work must be used for a single purpose—to further that understanding.* [pp. 118–119, italics added]

3. The interrelated methods of working inherent in an ego-psychological approach captured in the concept of the "working surface" (i.e., the state of the resistance, the degree of the ego's regression in thinking, ego autonomy, etc.) play little role in the relational model. The ego's widening capacity as a primary factor in the change process is eschewed, along with the role of interpretation in the bringing about the potential for structural change. Instead, analytic change is seen as located in the analysand's relational world. Insight is replaced by authenticity and meaning. The goal of analysis is to discover previously hidden parts of the self in the new experience with the analyst. The analyst and analysand discover and understand repetitive relational configurations in their interaction, while discovering new ways to relate to each other. Therapeutic action resides in the analyst's discovery of himself in these configurations, and what is therapeutic is "a gradual restructuring of the relationship on more collaborative terms" (Mitchell 1988, p. 301). Analysis of the patient's mind is de-emphasized, while the patient's experience of the analyst becomes a

prime focus of analysis. Since the analyst's subjectivity is an inevitable part of the analysis, its place in the analysis is heightened. As emphasized by Mitchell (1993),

> While not discounting the importance of early experiences, *this model locates the central mechanism of analytic change in an alternation in the basic structure of the analysand's relational world.* [p. 289, italics added]
>
> An interpretation is a *complex relational event*, not primarily because it alters something inside the analysand, not because it releases a stalled development process, but because it says something very important about where the analyst stands vis-à-vis the analysand, about what sort of relatedness is possible between them. [p. 295]

4. Is it the relationship that initiates the change process or interpretation? According to the relational perspective, no patient would stop resisting unless the analyst took over the affect-regulating components that allow for safety, or unless the analyst disconfirmed negative relational configurations. This is in contrast to those who believe the patient's greater freedom to think, feel, and experience (i.e., greater ego autonomy) is based on analysis of unconsciously motivated superego activities as demonstrated in resistances (Gray 1987, Kris 1990). In this latter model, the analyst's attempts to maintain a safe-enough relationship may inhibit analysis of ego restrictions. This particular issue is one that can be traced through analytic history (e.g., Sterba 1934, Strachey 1934) and in Freud's varying views on the topic.

My intent in this chapter is not to review the relational literature, but to focus solely on how its insights into the human condition and the analytic situation might be enhanced by considering an ego-psychological perspective.

In looking at the different models and the clinical techniques they lead to, I will emphasize the area that induced Freud to introduce the clinical construct of the ego—the analysis of unconscious resistances. It is fascinating to see that while there is general agreement among analysts of different stripes as to the mechanism underlying resistances (avoidance of unpleasant affect), the methods that evolve from this are quite different.

The view of resistances of the relational analyst Spezzano (1993) captures the important differences between a relational and ego-psychological perspective in approaching this clinical phenomenon. Spezzano's descriptions of the psychological reasons why resistances take place are consistent with how I've expressed it elsewhere (Busch 1992, 1995a):

> All people seek to avoid any engagement with the world and with other people that threatens to make them feel more anxious, more guilty, more ashamed than they already are. Patients will naturally and sensibly resist any effort on the part of the therapist to lead them into areas of their psychic and interpersonal life that they anticipate will make them feel any of the tension, distress, or pain they want to avoid. [Spezzano 1993, p. 184]

Then, in describing how these resistances need to be attended to first, Spezzano states that the analyst conveys his understanding of why "the patient is convinced that saying only what he says in exactly the way he says it constitutes his best chance to keep feeling good as he now feels rather than worse" (p. 186).

My views are similar:

> If a resistance is in operation, it indicates that the analysand is experiencing his thoughts or feelings as a danger. The purpose of the resistance is to keep the dangerous thought or feeling from awareness. The particular type of resistance is an adaptation, from an earlier time, to this threat. Interventions that do not respect the analysand's resistance to certain thoughts and feelings becoming conscious will be either irrelevant or potentially overwhelming. [Busch 1993, p. 168]

> Resistances are an adaptation to a threat to the ego at an earlier time. Thus, the patient who is silent in the face of emerging sexual thoughts about the analyst is not simply withholding, or derailing the process, or any of the other interpretations of hostility which may be part of the resistance. From the side of the ego resistance, the patient is responding to what is unconsciously experienced as a threat to which silence appears as a solution which mirrors an earlier adaptation. [Busch 1992, p. 1105]

It is striking, then, that even though Spezzano and I agree on one component of what resistances are attempting to accomplish (i.e., adaptation to a perceived threat), our views on the origin of this perspective are distinct. Thus, Spezzano (1993) sees Freud's theory of resistance analysis as moving increasingly away from the significance of affects, replaced by the resistance to remembering traumatic events. According to him, affective remembering became increasingly less important. "What matters is that the patient begins to connect previously unconnected thoughts, draws the right conclusions, and integrates isolated memories" (p. 192). Ego psychology is seen as an elaboration of Freud's (1914a) paper, "Remembering, Repeating and Working Through." He draws a line between analysts treating a resisting ego and those (like him) that treat an "affect-communicating subject" (p. 222).

My understanding of Freud is almost completely the opposite. Freud's move from the topographic to the structural model was based, in part, on his realization that there were powerful feelings that prevented patients from revealing themselves. These feelings, which were unconscious, were the nameless dangers and threats that led to the protective need to shut down or undo particular lines of inquiry. Thus the understanding of unconscious resistances was all about affects. In the Freudian model there is no resistance without powerful feelings. While the prestructural model was all about resistance to remembering, as captured in Freud's 1914 paper, his structural model was not increasingly about remembering. As noted by Jacobson (1993),

> Although structural psychoanalytic theory is frequently referred to in short-hand as drive-defense theory, that definition is actually geared to Freud's 1923 work, *The Ego and the Id*. With the addition of *Inhibitions, Symptoms and Anxiety* in 1926, and its later expansions, the theory became one of affective responses to intrapsychic wishes and their anticipated consequences, a theory of affect regulation in two senses: regulation *of* affect, and regulation *by* affect signals. [p. 538]

Thus, one cannot do resistance analysis from the ego-psychological perspective outlined here without treating an affective-
communicating subject. This is what the theory of resistance
analysis is all about—dangerous feelings. Thus, it seems highly
arbitrary to think one could distinguish a relational from an
ego-psychological approach on the basis that one theory pays
attention to affects while the other does not.

Spezzano's views on the complexity of the analyst's taking
in the patient's feelings, often before we are consciously aware
that something is occurring, speaks powerfully to an important component of working with resistances that has not been
adequately described in the literature on ego psychology. To
register these powerful, disturbing affects, and to hold on to
them long enough to say something useful about them without enacting some component of them, is a useful addition
to the understanding of the analyst's role in resistance analysis. The analysis is limited by the analyst's ability for affective
containment.

It is difficult to get a sense from Spezzano's writings on
resistance analysis just how he would work with resistances.
He gives no examples of specific resistance analysis, just a
general rendering of his position—a philosophical point of
view, not a technique. For example, in distinguishing his approach from the ego-psychological resistance approach, he
states,

> The holding, communicating, and interpretation of affect
> fully define the psychoanalytic situation and process. The
> analyst and analysand share the work of keeping alive, imagi-
> natively elaboratively, and thinking about the full range of

human affective states as these emerge in each of them during the analytic hours. [p. 229]

These sentiments are difficult to argue with, but how they
translate into the actual work of analysis is not specified.

Although not presented as an example of resistance analysis per se, we get a sense of how Spezzano works from his
presentation of the following vignette:

> Phil, a 19-year-old college student, found excitement pri-
> marily in exciting others. At one point in the treatment Phil
> was in conflict over whether to return to school. Spezzano
> sees his wishes to return based on a need to excite others
> (e.g., he captained and managed a sports team to which
> he felt indispensable), and a resistance to considering other
> possibilities. Spezzano challenges what he sees as Phil's
> defense by saying, "So, if you didn't return, they would
> close up shop and disband the team" (p. 170). He sees the
> patient's laugh as encouragement, and goes on in a similar
> vein. "I described his teammates sitting together and de-
> ciding that they were absolutely immobilized by his ab-
> sence" (p. 170). In this Spezzano sees himself as becom-
> ing "a less tragic and more comic conarrator of [the patient's
> story]" (p. 170). He believes his interventions "allowed him
> to put into perspective the question of how realistic it was
> to think that the excitement of his teammates would flow
> over and sustain him in academic work" (p. 170).

In this example, Spezzano has the view that the patient's
need to excite others is, in part, defensive. The analyst takes
on the role of regulating the patient's affect rather than ana-

lyzing the regulation process as a component of resistance analysis. He initiates a challenge to the patient's defense, and when he is encouraged by the patient's response he further challenges the defense. Thus, he becomes "a less tragic and more comic conarrator" (p. 170) of the patient's story. In this method the analyst first gauges the patient's readiness to have the defense challenged by challenging it, and then offers a more acceptable (i.e., less affectively disturbing) way to look at the patient's narrative as the sine qua non for further exploration. The analyst is working under the principle that of primary significance to the change process is his need to do something, and be a particular way, in order to allow the patient to more safely approach his defense. This is in contrast to my belief that while the analyst's timing, tact, and manner are of the utmost importance in any analytic process, working with the patient to recognize and understand the unconscious defensive processes is a major component of the freedom to think and feel, which is central to what analysis has to offer.

An ego-psychological approach suggests that the analyst's primary technical stance is not one of regulating the patient's affects via modeling or role playing in doing resistance analysis. Instead, the analyst evaluates the patient's readiness to approach disturbing feelings by listening closely to the patient's use of free association. This way the patient tells the analyst when he or she is ready. The patient uses signals to regulate affect, and a careful reading of these signals enables the analyst to determine the patient's readiness to deal with a defense. Also, there are different ways of approaching the resistances that utilize more or less of the patient's autonomous ego functions. One can invite or bypass these functions, which has important implications for the ego's capacity to regulate affect. For example, there must have been some sequencing of associations that led Spezzano to believe that the patient's need to excite others had a defensive quality. By bringing the associations to the patient's attention (e.g., "I wonder if you noticed that after you felt disappointed, you immediately began to describe how you tried to excite your teammates") we invite the ego's participation in the data of analysis as a method of understanding. We suggest that listening is a key to understanding those mechanisms that lead to the initiation of a defense. It is also a beginning investigation of why the patient might need the defense, which remains untouched in Spezzano's approach. This latter approach does not move toward understanding the psychological mechanisms underlying the need to excite.

In Spezzano's example the patient may end up feeling "more realistic" about his role with others as Spezzano suggests, but what led him to be unrealistic remains untouched. Nothing has been done to help the patient become less reliant on the analyst's affect containment. Further, the analyst hasn't helped the patient to know what he knows. This is an example of how different models of the mind lead to distinct clinical approaches to phenomena (e.g., resistances), even though there may be some similarities in how they are understood (e.g., adaptations). It is a scenario we will come upon often in comparing relational technique with that of ego psychology.

Although presented as part of his ongoing investigation into the relational perspective, Renik's (1995a) treatise on resistance analysis is consistent with most aspects of an ego-psychological perspective. His definition of a resistance (i.e., anything that interferes with self-awareness), his view that resistances analysis is based on the "facts of observation that are available and have been agreed upon by both analyst and analysand" (p. 88), and his stated goals for treatment (i.e., expansion of self-awareness) are all consistent with Gray's (1982, 1994) recent discussions of resistance analysis. While there are differences (e.g., Renik uses the term *resistance* as a descriptive clinical event rather than an intrapsychic process), I am more impressed with the areas of commonality. However, when we get to some of the clinical specifics there are important differences.

In Renik's (1996) paper on the problems with the concept of the analyst's neutrality, he presents a clinical report that highlights another distinct approach to resistances from a relational perspective.

A depressed woman believes her self-condemnations are based on her envious and hostile feelings toward her older sister who, she felt, got far greater attention from her parents because of a serious medical condition and poor school performance. In his comments to the patient, Renik challenges this perspective. "Without discrediting the sincerity of her feelings, I continued to question her sister as an object of resentment" (p. 501), believing that the patient's guilt over her hostility and envy

> might have the important defensive function of sparing her from experiencing serious criticisms of her parents and the accompanying awful feelings. Clearly, I was skeptical

about the emphasis placed on her envy, hostility, and guilt toward her sister. I was explicit with Diane about my judgments and the hypotheses they prompted. [pp. 501–502]

This brief vignette captures Renik's clinical approach to the patient's resistance to recognizing the hostility toward her parents. He believes Diane's feelings toward her sister are a defense against other feelings, and confronts this position with skepticism. It is consistent with a relational approach where changes are seen as taking place in the dialectic of the relationship. What the analyst offers in this case is "an alternative perspective, a new way of constructing reality" (p. 508). This is similar to Spezzano's manner of proceeding. It matters less that the analyst is right than that learning takes place in the patient's interaction with the analyst's position.

In contrast, an ego-psychological perspective would suggest that if one sees in the patient a threat against experiencing a feeling, one might try to demonstrate the existence of a resistance to the patient, and its adaptive meanings, before confronting or bypassing it. In this way one deals with the patient's, rather than the analyst's, awareness of a psychological process, while respecting the patient's reasons for the maintenance of the resistance. In contrast to Renik's earlier view that one best deals with resistances by agreed upon "facts of observation" (1995a, p. 88), in this case he is confronting the resistance by bringing in absent content (i.e., the patient's unconscious hostility toward her parents).

Again we see a difference from an ego-psychological approach, which suggests that one can see oscillation in the compromise formations in the patient's use of free association, and that the patient's co-participation in the process is enhanced by focusing on what is most observable rather than hypothesizing about absent content. For example, if there was a resistance to anger, Gray (1994) would expect to see it in such ways as the patient's expressing a hostile thought and then quickly moving away from it (e.g., "She made me really mad, but she was trying her hardest and who could fault her for that"). According to an ego-psychological perspective, it is in these observable moments of the patient's use of free association that resistances are most easily experienced and understood by the patient in an emotionally meaningful way. It is something the patient has just done, not something the analyst is saying the patient is doing. It is a method that suggests that major change processes take place in the ego; therefore, we need to include the ego as part of the process. By staying with what is most easily observable by the ego, we greatly enhance the ego's capacity to participate.

Renik's position, on the other hand, seems more dependent on his diagnosis of the situation and on confronting the patient's defenses against seeing the analyst's perspective. Renik says he "takes sides." What he takes sides about is the meaning of content, in contrast to those of us who focus more on the patient's use of the process of the associations. Renik attempts to show Diane whom she is really angry at. What I would attempt to show is that there is something dangerous to her in knowing about or expressing feelings of anger. In addition to differences in goals, there are different analytic frames. In Renik's view the key issue is what the analyst is thinking and feeling about what the patient is saying, in contrast to those of us who focus on bringing to the patients' attention what they are capable of observing in what they are saying.

Renik believes his work is similar to that of many analysts, and I would agree. In fact, Brenner similarly describes his way of dealing with a patient's defense against angry feelings, as described earlier. Brenner's view is based on the premise that a patient will continue to hold on to the defensive element of a compromise formation until one confronts the compromise formation. His view is based on the analyst's subjective reading of the patient's conflicts, in contrast to the patient's reading of the conflict. It is based on confronting the patient's view with the analyst's view.

While Renik's (1993) relational perspective on the analyst's subjectivity has helped us understand a previously warded-off component of the analyst's participation in the analytic process, I wonder if the "best way to avoid coercive influence and exploitation" (1995a, p. 85) is for the analyst to bring his values and constructs forward for mutual consideration. In the case of Diane, a woman who Renik believes is having difficulty knowing her own feelings (e.g., her anger toward her parents), is it most helpful for her to learn about her feelings by dealing with Renik's ideas on them? In contrast, Searl (1936) suggested, "That which is important is not the extent to which we may be able to impart to the patient our knowledge of his life and psyche, but it is the extent to which we can clear the patient's own way to it and give him freedom of access to his own mind" (p. 487). In general I have found that the tendency to confront a patient with feelings he or she is unaware of usually occurs when the defense is embedded in an unconscious attempt to actualize a fantasy. With certain patients the analyst's confrontation is part of an inevitable enactment that may be the first step in understanding. It is my impression that it may be easier for the analyst to withstand the pressure for enactments if he or she conceptualizes clear lines of intrapsychic demarcation between resistances and actualizations. Renik's (1995a) descriptive definition of resistances may lead to a blurring of this line.

While the points of agreement may ultimately outweigh those of disagreement, there are significant areas of difference between an ego-psychological and relational perspective in the integration of the analyst's subjective impressions. In dealing with the myriad thoughts and feelings the analyst has in any analytic session, relationalists seem more likely to share impressions, often before they themselves are sure of what they are saying or why they are saying it. It is part of the relational paradigm that patients will learn about themselves by dealing with the analyst's subjectivity. This is best exemplified in the following example from Aron (1996):

> A patient has been associating for some time about sadomasochistic interactions, and sexual fantasies of anal penetration and domination. Aron interprets that the patient believes Aron is controlling and dominating him. The patient confirms this, and then describes anal sadistic masturbatory fantasies. Aron then says
>
>> in a tone that I hope conveys that I am musing or thinking out loud, "The entire analysis is a sexual conquest for me, in which I become excited by your submission." I

leave ambiguous whether I mean this is his belief or fantasy or my own experience. As I say this to the patient, I may very well be unclear in whose voice I am speaking. The interpretation is not necessarily directed at him or me; it is not clear whose idea it is, and it may just as well lead to insight in me as to insight in him. If I do not dismiss all my patient's thoughts as projections or displacements from past objects, but instead consider that they may have some basis in my interaction with the patient, then in the very act of interpreting to the patient, I may learn something about myself and the analytic interaction. [p. 128]

I would characterize the differences between Aron's relational approach and mine in the following manner: Aron believes it is in doing something with the patient that the analyst finds out about his or her role in a possible enactment. "For example, as I tell the patient that I derive sexual excitement from dominating him, I may recognize some excitement in my tone of voice, excitement that I perhaps had not been aware of" (p. 128). In contrast, I would tend to focus on the patient's associations, my own associations, as well as the affective tone of my voice. Embedded in these different perspectives are two different models for self-awareness: one is in the interactional matrix, and the other is in listening to what is occurring in one's own mind. These differences are based, in part, in how much one believes awareness of emotional responses "necessarily follows translation of those responses into action" (Renik 1993, p. 556).

I believe that awareness of feelings does not require action, and this seems to be borne out by developmental studies that show thinking increasingly moving from its action roots (Piaget 1930, Piaget and Inhelder 1959). Thinking seems to become more action oriented in the face of conflict (Busch 1995b). Further, I think we need to consider the possible iatrogenic effect of leaving it ambiguous in our interpretation as to whether we are actually doing what the patient is fantasizing we are doing. There are powerful effects of fantasy on the patient's ability to deal effectively (in areas of conflict) with aspects of reality, because, in part, most conflicts derive from a time when thought and action were not that well separated, and in the midst of conflict this distinction is even further eroded. In this state, the analyst's leaving his intentions ambiguous could easily be traumatic. This is especially the case since there is no mention in Aron's account of taking into consideration the patient's readiness to grasp what he is doing. What Aron focuses on is his tone of voice, not the patient's state of readiness to hear. In fact there is an assumption in the relational perspective, and one that I believe is incorrect, that the patient's ego is ready to engage the analyst's perspective. I would suggest that even if the analyst's personal participation dominates the analysis, the patient's readiness to engage with this is severely limited (in a deeply emotional sense) for a long time. The emphasis in the relational literature is on the analysand's need to engage with the analyst, rather than on the patient's readiness to understand his or her need to do so.

As an experienced analyst I have no doubt that Spezzano, Renik, and Aron all have criteria for clinical judgments that lead them to work the way they do, including patients' readiness to work with their interpretation. It is the absence of any stated significance to an articulated sense of mind of the patient, except as the container of structural content, which, at times, leads their work to have such a retro (i.e., topographic) feel to it.

I believe there are certain interpretive guidelines the analyst might best follow in order to make his or her internal world clinically relevant for the patient. I would suggest that the analyst's subjective reactions will have little meaning to the patient unless these can be objectified. In short, our subjective reactions have to be objectified, in a concrete manner, into something the patient can see in his or her own associations, if it is to be usable information by the patient's ego. To make contact with that section of the ego turned toward the internal world, we must work through the part of the ego that is turned toward making sense of the external world. Also, as indicated earlier, the patient's thinking in areas of conflict leads to the need for concrete objectification of our subjective impressions, preferably in line with the patient's attempt at objectification of his or her subjective experience (i.e., the use of the method of free association), in order to be most immediately knowable by the patient.

We can do many other things with our subjective impressions. We can attempt to make the patient feel supported, safe, or appreciated, and these all may have their place and time in a treatment. However, from an ego-psychological perspective, certain changes can take place in analysis that define a psychoanalytic process. In part, it is changes in thinking that define the process, and this necessitates ways of working so that the state of the patient's ego is taken into account when using our subjective impressions for analytic interventions. In brief, to gain a sense of validity when considering the source of a seemingly spontaneously generated feeling or fantasy, I feel the need not only to listen to my own thoughts and feelings, but also to return to a close monitoring of the patient's association. Once it is determined that the feeling or fantasy is likely not the result of idiosyncratic musings, the patient's associations serve as an ideal vehicle for translation of subjective impressions into interventions that are understandable to a patient functioning at a concrete level of thinking. In short, there is a constant checking back and forth between my thoughts and the patient's associational mix (thoughts, actions, affects), to determine if there is congruence. For me, it is a basic part of the methodology of psychoanalytic work.

The difference between my way of working and that of the relationalists is exemplified in Himmelfarb's (1997) description of a similar debate in the discipline of history, put in a somewhat extreme form.

> For the postmodernist the very idea of the "discipline" of history, let alone of a methodology, is regarded as specious, even fraudulent. Where the modernist tries to overcome the ambiguity of "history" and bridge the gap between the past and the writing about the past, the postmodernist insists upon its radical, immutable ambiguity, the absolute disjunction between the past and any work about the past. Where the modernist, aware that there is no absolute truth, tries to arrive at the closest approximation to truth—to modest, contingent, tentative, incremental, proximate truths—the

postmodernist takes the denial of truth as a deliverance from any kind or degree of truth . . . . Where the modernist is challenged to try to achieve as much objectivity as possible, the postmodernist discredits the very idea of objectivity. Where the modernist, in short, tolerates relativism and tries to limit and control it, the postmodernist celebrates and exploits it. [pp. 147–148]

Here is an example of how I would work with a subjective impression:

Mr. A. has a Ph.D. in a social science. He is in his mid-30s. He began psychoanalysis after leaving a research fellowship in the second month because of an extreme sense of deprivation associated with needing to work long hours, a feeling of not being treated well by the director of the program, and severe bouts of anxiety when going to work in the morning. His quitting was only the latest in a series of sudden departures. He had left college in his first year, and returned to a university in his hometown. Graduate school, which he also attended in his hometown, took an extra two years as he left between his second and third years, and frequently dropped out for a semester. Mr. A.'s research position was his first attempt since college to leave the city he grew up in. From elementary through high school the patient was frequently absent, and always became ill when entering a new school.

Mr. A.'s parents were divorced when he was 3. He would often spend weekends with his father, who would involve him and his siblings in the father's chores (e.g., cleaning the father's apartment, and helping him wash his car). A constant part of the emotional landscape was the bevy of women gathered round the father. Mr. A.'s mother appeared to have severe narcissistic difficulties, alternately doting on and viciously attacking the patient.

Mr. A. obtained a less high-powered research position in business shortly after leaving the fellowship. He has remained in this position throughout the analysis, which is in its third year. The analysis has continued uninterrupted. The first two years of analysis were taken up with the protective qualities of his schizoid stance, a mirror of his life, and the multiple fears this protected him from. It is only recently he has referred to feelings about me as anything else than "here" (e.g., "I was working, feeling kind of down, when I thought about the upcoming break. I guess I must be missing 'here' "). The material to be presented is from the beginning of the third year of the analysis, chosen, in part, because it is typical of the way I work.

A feeling arises in the analyst, and it doesn't seem to fit the situation. What do we do with this subjective impression? How does it become clinically useful to the analysand?

It was summer, and had been raining for a number of days. The air was heavy with mist. Mr. A. began by noting the weather, and told of how it reminded him of fishing trips up north with his father. There was a wistful quality to Mr. A.'s voice when he said this, and he began to wax rhapsodically about past trips with his father.

I found myself feeling restless, and shifting around in my chair. In noting this I realized I was warding off a feeling of irritation with the patient. I scanned my thoughts to see what was coming to mind. I hadn't been aware of these feelings with other patients earlier in the morning. I then remembered Mr. A's rhapsodic tone. We had talked at length about his tendency to idealize these trips with his father. As the analysis went on, Mr. A. realized these trips occurred far less often than he remembered; there were frequent disagreements, and his father frequently left him alone. In part, the trips were remembered in idealized terms as a defense against the sadness, longing, and anger that he felt toward his father.

At this point I thought of the "boinging game," shorthand for a characteristic interaction between Mr. A. and his father. Shortly after the divorce, when at his father's house, Mr. A. would go to a door stop in the apartment, and continue to "boing" it until his father got furious at him. It seemed to have multiple purposes. On the one hand it was a turning of passive to active. It also seemed to be one of the few ways Mr. A. could get his father to respond to him. It would usually end with his father and Mr. A. apologizing to each other and hugging. This was one of the few moments of physical affection between them.

Was this what I was responding to? Was I being "boinged"? For what purpose? Was I avoiding my contribution to this? These were my thoughts at this point. I also noted I no longer felt irritated. It is an example of how when thoughts and feelings previously kept out of awareness can be given freer reign to consciousness, the propensity toward action (e.g., restlessness, irritation) can be changed to the possibility of reflection. I then listened for further associations to see if they confirmed any of these thoughts about my irritation, or set in motion new hypotheses. I believe we can frequently tell which of these ideas may be most correct primarily by listening to where the patient's thoughts go. It seems to me to be a necessary condition in fine-tuning what one's feelings are about in a manner that will be translatable to the patient. If it is an induced feeling in the analyst, how to help the patient take responsibility is the question. It is one of the most common yet trickiest issues in technique.

> Mr. A. then went on to talk about a phone call he had received the previous evening from an old friend whom he hadn't spoken to in a long time. In a continuation of his cheery voice, he told of how great this conversation was, but it was short on details and long on exclamations. He wound down these associations with the thought, "It was just like old times." Then, in a more reflective tone he wondered, "Why didn't we speak for three years?"

This is an important moment in the session, in that we see a change in Mr. A.'s relation to his own thoughts. For the first time in the session he is wondering about himself, and what has happened in this long absence. For me it is a moment when the patient's ego is more available for looking, thinking, and wondering. This is the concern that is available to him at this moment. It is the result of previous analytic work, so that Mr. A.'s reflective thinking can now be brought to bear on his own thought processes.

Mr. A. then went on to say that it was "simple" why he hadn't spoken with his old friend, at least from his side. He was irritated. He used to get into it with this friend all the time about who would call whom. He would keep track of these things, and finally he just got fed up because he felt he was the one who called all the time. This was all said with a sense of disbelief. It was as if the subtext was, "It's hard to hear what motivates me." There was then a momentary pause, and Mr. A.'s tone changed. With a sense of naive wonderment he exclaimed ecstatically how "amazing" it was that his friend had three children. Other words were also used to describe this, such as "incredible" and "fantastic."

I said to the patient that it seemed like he was becoming aware of the effect of his irritation on the distance he kept from his friend. He then seemed to suddenly distance himself from this feeling, and from his whole way of thinking about what he was saying. In this I am pointing to what the patient did with a thought (i.e., suddenly moved from it), as well as the patient's relationship to his own thoughts. It is a concrete, visible reality I am bringing to the patient's attention. He was talking about his irritation in this one way, then he briefly paused, and then suddenly talked and approached his talking in a whole new way. I purposefully left it up in the air as to whether this was a resistance, or an expression of the feelings of irritation. It was not clear which aspect Mr. A. was most ready to deal with at this point. The patient will tell us, via his associations, what he is ready to deal with.

Mr. A. found himself puzzled about the thoughts that were on his mind. They were actually some numbers. Then he realized they were the dates of my vacation, which I had mentioned the day before. He said, "The plot thickens!" He found himself thinking about Sarah yesterday. She is a woman with whom he has had a long-distance relationship for the past several months, with occasional weekend visits, as she lives in another city, several hours away. She is currently out of the country. When he was thinking about her yesterday, he briefly wondered if it had to do with my vacation. Then he forgot about it. He felt he missed Sarah, but ended up going to see a woman he recently met, and whiled away the afternoon "fooling around" in pre-coital seduction. He kept wondering what he was doing, and thought that if Sarah found out about this she would feel really bad. Maybe this was the point.

I said, "It seemed that fooling around with this woman was associated with warding off and expressing the thought that 'someone who was away would feel bad about this.' Your earlier thoughts suggested it was associated with my mentioning my vacation. But something about these feelings seemed dangerous as you needed to forget you had them." As I was talking he was thinking of himself in the coffee shop yesterday, and how his head would swivel around whenever an attractive woman would walk by. It was a carbon copy of how his father used to be when they went out together. He was probably intensely angry at these times. It was another way his father wasn't there. But he had to pretend that he wasn't angry. That's probably when he started on his career path of building "rafts for frogs," a reference to a recent session where this became a metaphor for his use of reaction formation. After he saw what he thought was a squashed frog in my driveway, which he then realized was a leaf, Mr. A. described in detail his respect for amphibians. He ended the current session by musing over his "raft building," and wondered, in a playfully sarcastic manner, when he would ever be able to fix that fatal flaw that causes the rafts to sink.

This session serves as a model for how I try to work with my subjective impressions, in this case a spontaneous feeling that seems based on a communication I am picking up unconsciously. First, I listen for some correlation between my associations and the patient's. Once I come to the conclusion there is some congruence, I wait to hear if there is something in the act or content of the patient's associations that allows me to point out that a feeling is being warded off. This allows for the pointing out of the resistance component of the compromise formation in its most concrete form. Once accomplished in the case just presented, we see there is less of a need for Mr. A. to disguise the feelings and their target (i.e., me).

The work on Mr. A.'s resistances to his anger and his feelings toward me had been ongoing for some time. When Mr. A.'s associations go to his "fooling around" with the woman he recently met, it is a choice point in the session. While there are suggestions of homoerotic feelings as part of the patient's feelings of irritation, this is further from the surface that the patient is closer to struggling with, that is, his actions as a compromise formation. By staying with what is most concrete, and closer to the surface, Mr. A. moves nearer to recognizing the hostility in his reaction formations. This is very different from where Mr. A. began the session, and it led to my feeling or irritation. That is, what could only be expressed in a subtle action by the patient saying "What a great guy my dad was," could increasingly be admitted into awareness. An important change has taken place in the ego. Shortly after this session, Mr. A. thought there might be a need for a new raft-building clientele—analysts.

In considering how the analyst uses his or her subjective impressions, we see contrasting clinical methods based on different views of the therapeutic task. I attempt to put the feelings I am having in the context of finding the "workable surface" to help the patient understand his own mind. At the time, he seemed not able to know of his anger toward me, leading him to need to express it unconsciously via action. This is what I was responding to. First and foremost, we are dealing with an *unconscious* resistance to a feeling state. My focus is on helping the patient see the existence of the resistance, and in this instance we can see how it led to his increasing freedom to be aware of his own feeling. While the task is defined in terms of freeing the patient's mind, there are other assumptions as part of this approach. Once the patient is freer to be aware of his anger, he now has the capability to choose to express it or not. Without this awareness he does not have the option. This has important relational consequences in terms of the expansiveness of his feelings, the freedom to act, and his authenticity in relationships. Both patients and analysts experience the enormous difference in their relational capacity after a resistance and the reasons for its existence have been understood, resulting in previously guarded-against feelings being allowed into awareness.

Aron's (1996) actions are based on his belief that enactments are inevitable, and that it is in the mutual analysis of them that change will occur, "with patient and analyst both interpreting as well as resisting the interpersonal meanings of their interactions and engagements" (p. 128). The assumption that the analyst is irreducibly subjective leads the relational analyst to more freely share his or her subjective impressions. In fact, it is an important part of what is presented as a less authoritarian stance. To do otherwise, according to this position, would lead the analyst to an inauthentically inhibited stance. If one's mind-set is that change occurs in the patient's dealing with the analytic relational configuration, then there is far greater leeway for the analyst's sharing the raw data of his or her subjectivity, in that everything becomes grist for the interactional mill.

What about those situations where the analyst isn't aware of a feeling until it is expressed? For example, the analyst hears something in his or her voice—a hostile edge, excessive kindliness, a seductive lilt. There are many areas one would have to know more about before deciding on a clinical approach. Do patients hear my voice in the same way I do? How conscious are they of hearing anything? Are they reacting to something but trying to keep it in the background? I believe these questions are approachable via what patients are doing with their associations. Is the patient who was freely associating suddenly silent? Is his or her voice now tight? Do the associations go to relevant content areas? Is there no discernible change in the content or affect? These are questions I would consider before knowing whether or how to approach the patient regarding what I had observed. While I have no doubt that the analyst's presence is always affecting the nature of the interaction in analysis, how available it is for consideration, how germane it is to what is on the patient's mind, in short, just how important it is to this patient's analysis at this time, are questions that would seem to separate ego-psychological and relational perspectives.

Two other object relations schools have struggled with similar issues. Levenson (1972, 1983), a leading interpersonal theorist, shows a familiar pattern in thinking about resistances in that while he has a descriptive view of resistances consistent with an ego-psychological perspective (e.g., "the patient has good reasons not to want to know, not to see what is there to be seen" (Levenson 1995, p. 3), his clinical technique is quite different. At the heart of Levenson's (1995) clinical technique is "a carefully framed detailed inquiry which mobilizes anxiety by looking where one is not supposed to look" (p. 4).

> The therapist locates these scotoma by looking for absences, omissions in the coherence of the patient's narrative. These "black holes" are the repository of anxiety and consequently of those issues and experiences which are being excluded from awareness. [p. 3]

The purpose, according to Levenson, "is to deconstruct the story, locate the omissions and investigate them" (p. 3).

As one can see, the absence of an intrapsychic model leads Levenson to a different approach to the resistances. It is based on a belief, in part, that anxiety is an interpersonal event, and that defenses are formed against other people and not a patient's own unconscious thoughts or feelings. However, this approach does not seem to touch the issue of why the threat of looking into areas is there in the first place. It is the differences between believing there is already anxiety there and helping the patient see those signs of resistance that indicate anxiety is present, and seeing the analyst's job as mobilizing anxiety. It is the difference between, on the one hand, seeing the analyst's job as deconstructing the story and, on the other, helping the patient (1) understand the presence of something to be deconstructed, (2) understand why they have not been able to deconstruct their own story, and then (3) deconstruct it.

If patients leave something out of their narrative, or are unclear about a particular aspect of it, I would tend to see what the patients' associations may tell us about the lack of clarity, or what the purpose was of something being left out. If I raise a question about some piece of information being left out, its purpose is to direct the patient's attention to the lack of clarity, not to get the information. In fact it has been my impression that in such a situation a patient is more likely to want to reveal the missing information than notice the process of concealment.

Levenson's more active pursuit of issues on the analyst's agenda seems not designed to bring about what he states is the intended effect of such an inquiry, that is, that "patients understand that their singularity and privacy are respected"

(p. 3). His view is based on the notion that patients will appreciate the analyst's finding out as much as possible, and not treating them like generic analysands. However, while patients need to be treated and viewed in their unique ways, true respect and privacy may come more from the analyst's appreciation of the ego's need to keep certain material out of awareness until it feels safe to do so, and not because of the analyst's agenda.

It was interesting to see Levenson (1997) grapple with some of these contradictions in a recent workshop. In response to a discussion in which an analyst described bringing something to the patient's attention from a chance meeting outside of the analytic hour, Levenson offered that this is something he wouldn't do. He felt to do so was being a "poor sport." In elaboration he explained that since the patient didn't invite or initiate the interaction, it is not being respectful of the patient's autonomy. Yet, it seems to me that Levenson does not show this same level of sportsmanship in the analytic hours. This is how his approach differs from an ego-psychological one. He seems to assume the patient's being in the office is an invitation to intervene.

I would suggest that one has to listen carefully to determine when one is being invited to participate in a discussion of the patient's internal or interpersonal world. Levenson's perspective is based on ferreting out the content areas where a patient is anxious, while mine is based on the analyst's respect for the anxiety already there, which leads to an opposite view of the basic frame of the analysis. Thus Levenson (1995) describes how, in beginning a treatment, there are certain areas that are vital to explore: how the patient came to the analyst, the patient's view of cure, and what the patient wants. This is a very different model for beginning an analysis than one I had proposed (Busch 1995c). I believe that issues can only be meaningfully explored in an analytic fashion when the patient is ready. If the issue is a conflictual one for the patient, and the resistances have been worked with, then an exploration of issues can take place with the full, emotional participation of the analysand. Certainly other modes of exploration can take place. However, when goals of analysis differ, methods of intervention will also vary. From my perspective, with analyzable patients there is little that is vital to get to until it becomes something the patient is ready to deal with.

There are distinct ways in which the analyst participates in the analytic process. Levenson, like many analysts associated with the schools of object relations, tends to take a more active role in the analytic process than an ego-psychological approach would dictate. This is true about asking questions, sharing fantasies or feelings, and determining what is really going on with the patient. He seems less concerned with the "workable surface" (i.e., that material available to be worked with by the conscious ego), and more attuned to the "analytic surface" (i.e., the analyst's own thoughts and ideas about what is occurring). The analyst participates at a different level regarding both the degree of direction of the patient's thoughts and the places where we might intervene.

Among those associated with an object relations perspective, Kohut was the most ambivalent about an ego-psychological perspective. While many of Kohut's views on the psychologi-

cal consequences of narcissistic disorders seem to fit comfortably within an ego-psychological perspective and were embraced by Kohut on this level, at other times the contributions
of ego psychology were dismissed. On the positive side, Kohut
(1984) could state, "With reference to the issue of cure, the
continuity between ego psychology and self psychology is most
palpable" (p. 95). Without identifying it as such, he took
generously from the principles underlying ego psychology.
How ready he was to recognize its significance in the psychoanalytic process depended, it seemed, on how ready he was
to see self psychology as "complementary" (p. 65) to other
perspectives. His negative views of ego psychology were based
on prevailing misconceptions that did not take into account
the significance of resistance analysis, and the role of the
autonomous ego functions. Yet, Kohut and Wolf's (1978)
illuminating descriptions of interferences in narcissistic development and their consequences for psychic functioning are invaluable to our understanding of a whole range of threats to
the ego's sense of well-being, which lead to significant resistances not understandable with any other model. For example,
those patients who become threatened when feeling stimulated
are understandable within a model of faulty idealizing, while
the mirroring transference also brings clarity to previously un-
explained resistance in the analytic setting.

However, at other times Kohut sees ego psychology as adding little to the theory of technique and clinical psychoanalysis. Kohut (1984) states, "For purposes of reexamining the
concepts of defense and resistance, moreover, even the theoretical modifications introduced by ego psychology are of little

consequence" (p. 113). He equated the ego-psychological method with "the penetration-to-the-unconscious-via-the-over-coming-of resistance model" (p. 113). In fact, as we have seen with most of the object relations schools, his view of resistances was exactly the same as an ego-psychological one, this time with a self-psychological twist:

> They constitute valuable moves to safeguard the self, how-ever weak and defensive it may be, against destruction and invasion. It is only when we recognize that the patient has no healthier attitude at his disposal than the one he is in fact taking that we can evaluate the significance of "defenses" and "resistances" appropriately. [p. 141]

Kohut is basing his view of resistances on Freud's (1926) second theory of anxiety without labelling it as such. What he has added is another possible threat the ego may be re-sponding to, a threat to the self. Further, his description of resistances as "adaptive and psychologically valuable" (p. 114) was first developed within ego psychology, and is inherent within an approach to resistance analysis based on this model. Kohut's emphasis on the adaptive components of resistances is a reaction, in part, to what I believe he accurately perceived as a "morality-tinged scientific model about the need to make the unconscious conscious" (p. 141). Kohut's view of resis-tances as a danger or threat is entirely consistent with an ego-psychological approach, except in this latter approach the po-tential threats to be considered are most encompassing.

It is surprising that to this day self psychologists believe they have discovered resistances as "the best, indeed the only, adaptive means of self protection available to a patient at a given point in time" (Malin 1993, p. 506), while relegating what is called traditional methods of resistance analysis to "blunting or inhibiting conflicts arising from developmentally determined instinctual sources" (p. 516). Rabin (1995), in an article extolling what he describes as the liberating effects of the paradigm shifts in therapeutic technique inherent in the self-psychological and interpersonalist approaches, inaccurately depicts an ego psychological approach in Reichian terms, as a "battle cry to join with her 'healthier ego' and do battle with the powerful forces of her resistances" (p. 477). It is a prestructural model of dealing with resistances that Freud struggled with even after the introduction of his second theory of anxiety (Gray 1982, Busch 1992). What Rabin views as the humanizing effects on treatment of a paradigm shift is the shift inherent in an ego-psychological approach. What Rabin and others are responding to, as noted earlier, is that this shift was never fully integrated into psychoanalytic technique.

Wolf (1988), like Kohut, has a view of resistance analysis that is similar to that of an ego-psychological perspective. This can be seen in this pithy summary which could come straight from a textbook on ego psychology: "For in essence, resistance is nothing but fear of being traumatically injured again" (p. 111). The major difference is that Wolf sees the threat as narrowly defined to a fragile sense of self or protection of a selfobject relationship. In the self-psychological model the analyst's goal in his use of the method of free association is an empathic attunement with the patient's feeling state, for the purpose of repairing the inevitable disruptions that occur in this process. This leads to a very different use of, and perspective on, the patient's use of free association. Associations seem to be viewed as veridical representations of feeling states (see Ornstein and Ornstein 1994) rather than thoughts that are coming to mind that reflect one component or another of a compromise formation, psychic structure, or feeling state about the sense of self. The goals are different from when free association is used to help free the patient to hear and observe what is on his on her mind as a way of understanding disruptions in functioning. In this latter model there is a mind that changes; in the former the patient's mind is not a particularly important part of the process. Thus, for Wolf, the ambiance is "more important than the exact verbal content of the resistance interpretation" (p. 111).

In summary, the schools of object relations have offered important correctives to our understanding of relationships in the formation and amelioration of pathology. These areas had been underemphasized in previous elaborations of the structural model. On the other hand, it is important to note that these models involve basic changes in clinical technique around what is being understood, and how it is being understood. From an ego-psychological perspective, these theories do not take sufficient account of the concept of the patient's mind, and thus are not able to pay sufficient attention to the concept of the patient's workable surface. Ignored is the ego's integrative capacities as demonstrated in the use of free association. Finally, while these schools have been in the forefront of alerting us to the authoritarian tilt inherent in classical psychoanalysis, their methods, at times, seem likely to bring about this very same tilt (e.g., the detailed inquiry). The concept of the analyst's inevitable subjectivity seems to lead to a position where the analysand is asked to come to grips with the analyst's personality rather than the analyst coming to grips with the analysand's. However, I want to emphasize the depth of understanding these schools have brought to the clinical enterprise, and the many important questions they raise. I hope that the issues raised here from an ego-psychological perspective are taken in the spirit of further inquiry.

7

Multiple Causes, Multiple Functions

This is a time of great professional and intellectual ferment in psychoanalysis. Barriers between professional groups, fortified by decades of elitism and mistrust, are beginning to crumble, leading to an invigorated debate on the important issues facing clinical psychoanalysis. It is my impression that this is being done in an atmosphere of increasing openness to new ideas. It is a propitious time to rethink a conceptual framework (i.e., an ego-psychological approach to clinical technique) we mistakenly believed dominated American psychoanalysis when indeed, at best, it has only been a rudimentary form of this method. Further, the movement to turn the psychoanalytic paradigm into an interactional one suffers, I believe, from inattention to ego-psychological considerations, leading to a method that, at times, repeats the errors it is attempting to correct.

We need to rethink our clinical technique in the light of ego psychology for the following reasons:

1. Ego psychology has important clinical utility. During a successful analysis significant changes take place in the autonomous ego functions. This can be seen in the increased capacity to allow thoughts to come into consciousness; the ability to reflect upon those thoughts; and a decrease in the intensity of previously crippling affects, with an accompanying freedom to experience a range of feelings. Given the above, those clinical methods that foster and detract from ego autonomy need to be identified and become part of our conceptualization of clinical technique.

2. If one believes that there is a mind with deeply embedded structures that play a significant role in how patients think about themselves, about others, and about their own thinking, then taking these structures into account as part of our clinical technique becomes a sine qua non of treatment. At this stage of our field we have just skimmed the surface in this area, and are only beginning to use insights like Sandler's (1975) observation that we tend to neglect the *"dominant modes of unconscious childhood cognition which persist in the present and which are still utilized in the present"* (p. 376, emphasis original).

3. The concept of a *workable surface* is invaluable in accounting for the multiple factors, mediated by the patient's ego, that allow for the use of an intervention, and as a guarantee of the ego's autonomy.

4. The ego's functioning as a guiding light in our interpretive stance offers a framework for understanding the use of the process versus the use of content. Resistance analysis is a prime example of this.

From another perspective, the issues that bring patients into treatment are inevitably revived in the transference in a fully developed analysis. These are invariably due to multiple factors. The more factors that can be brought to the patient's awareness in a manner usable by the ego, the better the chance for the patient to weather the inevitable pull of regressive tendencies. This is a major reason why it is necessary for an analyst to have a broad-based understanding of behavior.

At the same time that a patient is exposing the various factors that led to his or her symptoms, the multiple functions underlying these symptoms are being expressed in the transference. At one moment the patient is resisting the awareness of an unconscious fantasy, while at another moment the same behavior may unconsciously express the fantasy in action. For example, a patient growing silent after expressing a competitive thought toward the analyst may be retreating from the thought, while at another time silence may be an attempt to defeat the analyst.

The failure of the major psychoanalytic theories is that each is limited in its receptivity to alternative perspectives. Further, none has sufficiently taken into account the role of the ego as a type of gatekeeper of the affect-regulating cognitive soul, and as a major component of the change process. It is through the ego that we reach others, and it is the ego that protects one's basic sense of self while attempting to find ways to express it. Interpretations can only be usable if understandable, acceptable, and meaningful to the ego. The structural model, as currently interpreted, is the one theory that accounts for the multiple functions of behaviors (i.e., compromise formations), but it has been limited in the breadth of acceptable causative factors.

In rethinking clinical technique we need to keep an open mind to those causative factors that determine behaviors, while paying greater attention to what we need to understand about the ego's readiness to participate in the process of understanding. With regard to the first point, over the course of an analysis it should not surprise us to find that a typical transference from any patient has elements in it that are best understood within a multiplicity of frameworks. The same broad-based understanding must be applied to what is curative in the psychoanalytic process. In many ways we have seemed like the blind men describing an elephant—each of us elucidating a piece of the process and thinking of it as the whole. While we may think of essential elephantness in terms of its floppy ears, trunk, size, and apparent gentle demeanor, there can be no elephant without a torso, legs, and eyes. In a similar vein, while the patient's sense of safety in the treatment may not define psychoanalysis, it is difficult to imagine a fully realized psychoanalytic treatment without the patient feeling safe enough. On the other hand, the patient's safety is not all of psychoanalysis. An ego-psychological perspective has not been applied to those elements of the psychoanalytic process I would consider necessary but not sufficient to describe psychoanalysis (i.e., its legs and torso). It is to some of these areas I now turn.

I will start with the issue of the authenticity of the analysis. We inevitably make errors in treatment. These include errors in understanding and errors in relating. For example, the analyst's saying something hurtful to a patient, even if it is in response to an unconscious perception that ultimately may be helpful, is still an error and will be understood by the patient as such. Our capacity to experience, absorb, and use affects that at the very least may be unpleasant to us has much to do with how authentically the patient may be able to experience the analysis. If in our role of analyst we are not able to do what we are asking the patient to do, that is, understand the threat associated with certain thoughts and feelings in order to open one's mind to all that may be there, then the entire process has a ring of inauthenticity. If we are unable to tolerate a certain degree of painful affect in our relationship with patients, then from what position are we asking them to tolerate a certain discomfort in order to seek out its causes? By not acknowledging our errors we are asking patients to deny what they have just seen. It is as if we are saying to patients, "While you think you saw something about me, you really didn't." In a treatment where the purpose is to help patients find free access to any thought they may have, we are closing off an area that is an important component of their feeling about the treatment.

An ego-psychological perspective gives us another route into understanding the significance of the analyst's acknowledging mistakes, and its role in the authenticity of the treatment.[1] The above scenario is just one of the many ways the authenticity of the analysis is established. For example, consistent rigidification of interpretation or technique, leading the analyst to not understand such things as the distinction between creative rebellion and cruel dismissal, or a gift of appreciation versus a gift of seduction, also has a stultifying effect on the authenticity of the analysis.

---

1. I am simplifying a most complex issue. There are endless subtleties to what we do in the treatment, and what the patient notices. One may pay more or less attention to a potential analytic error depending on the state of the transference. A sadomasochistic transference, where the helpful aspects of the treatment are overwhelmed by the patient's endless picking at the details, may lead to a different scenario from the one indicated above.

Another component of what might be considered a necessary but not sufficient component of an analysis (i.e., the torso of the elephant) is the degree to which patients feel the analyst is interested in and concerned about them. It is difficult to imagine patients fully committing themselves to an increasingly free exploration of themselves with an analyst consistently experienced as distant, unconcerned, or self-absorbed. Yet feeling the opposite is not equivalent to having an analytic experience. Further, the analyst's expression of interest and concern can primarily be conveyed by the manner in which the analyst analyzes, and not necessarily by the introduction of extra-analytic parameters. The analyst's attempt to listen carefully to the patient in a respectful manner, along with the capacity to understand and convey this understanding in a way the patient can find useful, goes a long way toward conveying the analyst's interest and concern. For example, if the analyst is able to convey his belief in the patient's use of free association, the issue of why the analyst doesn't answer questions immediately becomes a less charged one. That is, if the analyst is able to convey he is interested in everything that comes to the patient's mind, and truly follows that principle in his or her work, questions become another thought coming to the patient's mind (as well as a reality that may need to be spoken to at some time).

It is primarily when patients don't understand the purpose of free association, as for example when the analyst conveys the impression that the patients' thoughts are a vehicle for the analyst's expressing his or her clinical acumen, intuition, or empathy, that waiting for the patients' associations after they ask a question becomes for patients a type of toilet-training experience. From what I hear in clinical discussions, analysts seem to be increasingly thinking that answering patients' questions is an antidote to the stereotypic uncaring analyst. This is usually presented under the theoretical banner of the analyst's being less authoritarian. Yet, there is nothing inherently more or less authoritarian about answering questions, as it all depends on the context in which it occurs. For example, to treat the patient's request for a time change only as an association may very well be to ignore the importance of her reality in a preemptive manner. On the other hand, the analyst telling the patient where he or she is going on summer vacation may, for a narcissistically vulnerable patient who felt the need to mirror her parents, reenact an aspect of a pathological relationship under the guise of being more open. In short, there are many components that make a psychoanalysis possible. Some may be necessary for psychoanalysis to occur but not sufficient to define a psychoanalysis, while others may be necessary and sufficient. We have, at times, not kept these two ways of thinking about the psychoanalytic process separate enough. An ego-psychological perspective adds immeasurably to both elements.

What seems immutably psychoanalytic is the role of the unconscious in psychological functioning. In its simplest form we see the patient guided by various unconscious thoughts that, when they approach awareness, result in an unconscious sense of danger leading to a variety of compromise formations. The discovery of the unconscious, and its importance in psychic life, is what has defined psychoanalysis from its inception.

I cannot imagine a successful analysis without a full exploration of the manner in which unconscious fantasies drive the patient's difficulties. It is what I would define as a necessary and sufficient component of psychoanalysis. It is mildly ironic that when I consider what is an essential part of the psychoanalytic process, I return to Arlow and Brenner's notion of exploring the unconscious fantasies and compromise formations. However, I have not disagreed with the interpretive content they consider essential, only with the manner in which they have gone about it and a certain narrowness to their focus. An ego-psychological perspective serves as a useful model from which to investigate unconscious functioning in that it is the only model that takes into account the two sides of the ego, one of which is turned inward to gauge safety and/or danger, and the other is turned outward to understand information from the external world and integrate it with what is unconsciously perceived. One will value it or not, depending on the importance one finds for the concept of a mind with multiple layers of structure.

We need to further explore the realm of the ego and clinical technique. This area has never been easy for psychoanalysts to accept. Anna Freud (1966), in commenting on the extraordinary opposition to Hartmann's early work in ego psychology, stated,

> But, above all, there were many who feared that the explicit introduction of an ego psychology into psychoanalysis endangered its position as a depth psychology, a discipline concerned exclusively with the activity of the instinctual drives and the functioning of the unconscious mind. Taking the

stand that work on the ego was an unwarranted extension
of analysis, they ignored the fact that, from its beginnings,
psychoanalytic metapsychology was intended to embrace all
the agencies within the mental apparatus plus their interactions. [p. 17]

Anna Freud went on to describe how, at the time of her talk,
she felt Hartmann's ideas had been well accepted. However,
her conclusion now seems premature. It is not a novel idea
to suggest that today, still, beyond the mandatory institute
course in ego psychology, most psychoanalysts have devoted
little time to the topic of the ego in clinical technique. While
previously it was the instincts that analysts feared would be
ignored by the new ego psychology, currently it is the realm
of the relationship.

It is amusing to think of the concerns about ego psychology deflecting from the instincts at a time when it was thought
that the deepest layers of the mind had been penetrated within
the three to six months analyses lasted. It has been my experience that before actually hearing how an ego-psychological
approach can be applied to clinical technique, concerns exist
among many analysts about the method being too cognitive
or intellectualized. I have suggested historical reasons for this
(Busch 1993), but it also has to do with psychoanalysts confusing the cognitive and the intellectualized. Taking into account more of what is tolerable to the patient's conscious
mind, while also relying more on what Friedman (1989) described as old-fashioned intelligence is not the same as the
treatment becoming intellectualized. When an ego-psychological approach is undertaken within the context of a respectful,

humane relationship, with an appreciation for the complexities of human behavior and our own limitations in understanding it, it leads to a deepening of feelings and their understanding—in the patient, in the analyst, and in the relationship between the two. Further, there is nothing in what I have said that contradicts Friedman's telestic summation of the complexities of the analytic task:

> I think we would assign the patient a task, but rather casually so as not to pin our hopes on it. We would encourage rational self-examination while expecting it to serve non-rational, often obscure purposes. Doggedly trying to bring understanding to everything that comes before us, we would yet not be demoralized by inklings that the patient's understanding is a double agent. On the contrary, our determination would be strengthened because we would see that duplicity as multilevel problem-solving. [p. 549]

References

Abend, S. (1982). Serious illness in the analyst: countertransference considerations. *Journal of the American Psychoanalytic
Association* 30:365–380.

Arlow, J. A. (1969). Unconscious fantasy and the disturbance of
conscious experience. *Psychoanalytic Quarterly* 38:1–27.

——— (1979). Metaphor and the psychoanalytic situation. *Psychoanalytic Quarterly* 48:363–386.

——— (1985). The concept of psychic reality and related problems.
Journal of the American Psychoanalytic Association 33:521–536.

——— (1987). The dynamics of interpretation. *Psychoanalytic
Quarterly* 56:68–87.

——— (1995). Stilted listening. *Psychoanalytic Quarterly* 64:215–
233.

Arlow, J. A., and Brenner, C. (1964). *Psychoanalytic Concepts and
Structural Theory*. New York: International Universities Press.

——— (1990). The psychoanalytic process. *Psychoanalytic Quarterly* 59:678–692.

Aron, L. (1996). *A Meeting of Minds*. Hillsdale, NJ: Analytic Press.

Bion, W. (1959). Attacks on linking. *International Journal of Psycho-
Analysis* 40:308–315.

——— (1962). *Learning from Experience*. New York: Basic Books.

Brenner, C. (1976). *Psychoanalytic Technique and Psychic Conflict.* New York: International Universities Press.

—— (1979). Working alliance, therapeutic alliance, and transference. *Journal of the American Psychoanalytic Association* 27:137–157.

—— (1982). *The Mind in Conflict.* Madison, CT: International Universities Press.

—— (1994). The mind as conflict and compromise formation. *Journal of Clinical Psychoanalysis* 3:473–488.

—— (1995). Some remarks on psychoanalytic technique. *Journal of Clinical Psychoanalysis* 4:413–428.

Busch, F. (1989). The compulsion to repeat in action: a developmental perspective. *International Journal of Psycho-Analysis* 70:535–544.

—— (1992). Recurring thoughts on unconscious ego resistances. *Journal of the American Psychoanalytic Association* 40:1089–1115.

—— (1993). In the neighborhood: aspects of a good interpretation and a "developmental lag" in ego psychology. *Journal of the American Psychoanalytic Association* 41:151–177.

—— (1994). Some ambiguities in the method of free association and their implications for technique. *Journal of the American Psychoanalytic Association* 42:363–384.

—— (1995a). *The Ego at the Center of Clinical Technique.* Northvale, NJ: Jason Aronson.

—— (1995b). Do actions speak louder than words?: A query into an enigma in analytic theory and technique. *Journal of the American Psychoanalytic Association* 43:61–82.

—— (1995c). Beginning a psychoanalytic treatment: establishing an analytic frame. *Journal of the American Psychoanalytic Association* 43:449–468.

—— (1995d). Resistance analysis and object relations theory: erroneous conceptions amidst some timely contributions. *Psychoanalytic Psychology* 12:43–53.

—— (1996). The ego and its significance in analytic interventions. *Journal of the American Psychoanalytic Association* 44:1073–1099.

—— (1997). Understanding the patient's use of the method of free association: an ego psychological approach. *Journal of the American Psychoanalytic Association* 45:407–424.

Davison, W., Pray, M., and Bristol, C. (1990). Mutative interpretation and close process monitoring. *Psychoanalytic Quarterly* 59:599–628.

Erikson, E. H. (1950). *Childhood and Society.* New York: Norton.

Fenichel, O. (1941). *Problems of Psychoanalytic Technique.* New York: Psychoanalytic Quarterly.

Freud, A. (1936). *The Ego and the Mechanisms of Defense.* New York: International Universities Press.

—— (1965). Diagnostic skills and their growth in psychoanalysis. *International Journal of Psycho-Analysis* 46:31–38.

—— (1966). Links between Hartmann's ego psychology and the child analyst's thinking. In *Psychoanalysis—A General Psychology*, ed. R. M. Lowenstein, L. M. Newman, M. Schur, and A. Solnit, pp. 16–27. New York: International Universities Press.

Freud, S. (1895). Studies on hysteria. *Standard Edition* 2.

—— (1900). The interpretation of dreams. *Standard Edition* 4.

—— (1912). The dynamics of the transference. *Standard Edition* 12:97–108.

—— (1914a). Remembering, repeating, and working through. *Standard Edition* 12:145–156.

—— (1914b). On narcissism: an introduction. *Standard Edition* 14:67–104.

—— (1917). Introductory lectures on psychoanalysis, XXVI. *Standard Edition* 16.

—— (1923). The ego and the id. *Standard Edition* 19:3–68.

—— (1926). Inhibitions, symptoms and anxiety. *Standard Edition* 20:77–178.

—— (1933). New introductory lectures on psychoanalysis, XXXI. *Standard Edition* 22.

Friedman, L. (1969). The therapeutic alliance. *International Journal of Psycho-Analysis* 50:139–153.

—— (1984). Pictures of treatment by Gill and Schafer. *Psychoanalytic Quarterly* 53:167–207.

—— (1989). Hartmann's *Ego Psychology and the Problem of Adaptation*. *Psychoanalytic Quarterly* 58:526–550.

Goldberger, M. (1996). *Danger and Defense: The Technique of Close Process Monitoring*. Northvale, NJ: Jason Aronson.

Gray, P. (1982). "Developmental lag" in the evolution of technique for psychoanalysis of neurotic conflict. *Journal of the American Psychoanalytic Association* 30:521–655.

—— (1987). On the technique of the analysis of the superego—an introduction. *Psychoanalytic Quarterly* 56:130–154.

—— (1992). Memory as resistance and the telling of a dream. *Journal of the American Psychoanalytic Association* 40:307–326.

—— (1994). *The Ego and Analysis of Defense*. Northvale, NJ: Jason Aronson.

Greenberg, J., and Mitchell, S. A. (1983). *Object Relations and Psychoanalytic Theory*. Cambridge, MA: Harvard University Press.

Greenson, R. R. (1967). *The Technique and Practice of Psychoanalysis*, vol. 1. New York: International Universities Press.

Hartmann, H. (1939). *Ego Psychology and the Problem of Adaptation*. New York: International Universities Press, 1958.

———— (1950). Comments on the psychoanalytic theory of the ego. In *Essays on Ego Psychology*, pp. 113–141. New York: International Universities Press, 1964.

———— (1952). The mutual influences in the development of ego and id. In *Essays on Ego Psychology*, pp. 155–181. New York: International Universities Press, 1964.

———— (1955). Notes on the theory of sublimation. *Psychoanalytic Study of the Child* 10:9–29. New York: International Universities Press.

Hartmann, H., and Kris, E. (1945). The genetic approach in psychoanalysis. *Psychoanalytic Study of the Child* 1:11–30. New York: International Universities Press.

Hartmann, H., Kris, E., and Loewenstein, R. M. (1946). Comments on the formation of psychic structure. *Psychological Issues* 14:27–55.

Himmelfarb, G. (1997). "Beyond method." In *What's Happened to the Humanities?* ed. A. Kernan, pp. 143–161. Princeton, NJ: Princeton University Press.

Hoffman, I. Z. (1983). The patient as interpreter of the analyst's experience. *Contemporary Psychoanalysis* 19:389–422.

———— (1987). The value of uncertainty in psychoanalytic practice. *Contemporary Psychoanalysis* 23:205–215.

———— (1992). Some practical implications of a social-constructivist view of the analytic situation. *Psychoanalytic Dialogues* 2:287–304.

Holmes, D. (1996). Emerging indicators of ego growth and associated resistances. *Journal of the American Psychoanalytic Association* 44:1101–1119.

Holt, R. R. (1972). Freud's mechanistic and humanistic views of man. In *Psychoanalysis and Contemporary Science, vol. 1*, ed. R. R. Holt and E. Peterfreund, pp. 3–24. New York: Macmillan.

Jacobs, T. (1997). Response to the contributors to "Essays Inspired by Theodore Jacobs's *The Use of the Self*." *Psychoanalytic Inquiry* 17:108–119.

Jacobson, J. G. (1993). Developmental observation, multiple models of the mind, and the therapeutic relationship in psychoanalysis. *Psychoanalytic Quarterly* 62:523–552.

Kernberg, O. (1976). *Borderline Conditions and Pathological Narcissism*. Northvale, NJ: Jason Aronson.

Kleban, C. H. (1994). Transference manifestations as changing compromise formations throughout an analysis: a contribution to the discussion of transference resistance and transference. *Journal of Clinical Psychoanalysis* 3:429–451.

Kohut, H. (1984). *How Does Analysis Cure?* Chicago, IL: University of Chicago Press.

Kohut, H., and Wolf, E. S. (1978). The disorders of the self and their treatment. *International Journal of Psycho-Analysis* 59:414–425.

Kramer, Y. (1988). In the visions of the night: perspectives on the work of Jacob A. Arlow. In *Fantasy, Myth, Reality*, ed. H. P. Blum, Y. Kramer, A. K. Richards, and A. D. Richards, pp. 9–40. Madison, CT: International Universities Press.

Kris, A. O. (1982). *Free Association: Method and Process*. New Haven, CT: Yale University Press.

——— (1990). Helping patients by analyzing self criticism. *Journal of the American Psychoanalytic Association* 38:605–636.

Levenson, E. A. (1972). *The Fallacy of Understanding*. New York: Basic Books.

——— (1983). *The Ambiguity of Change*. New York: Basic Books.

——— (1993). Shoot the messenger: interpersonal aspects of the analyst's interpretations. *Contemporary Psychoanalysis* 29:383–396.

——— (1995). A monopedal presentation of interpersonal psycho-analysis. *Review of Interpersonal Psychoanalysis* 1:1–4.

——— (1997). Two-day clinical workshop. Meetings of the American Psychoanalytic Association, San Diego, CA, May.

Levy, S., and Inderbitzen, L. B. (1990). The analytic surface and the theory of technique. *Journal of the American Psychoanalytic Association* 38:371–392.

Loewald, H. W. (1971). Some considerations on repetition and repetition compulsion. *International Journal of Psycho-Analysis* 52:59–66.

Loewenstein, R. M. (1950). Ego development and psychoanalytic technique. In *Practice and Precept in Psychoanalytic Technique: Selected Papers of R. M. Loewenstein*, pp. 30–39. New Haven, CT: Yale University Press, 1982.

——— (1952). Some remarks on the role of speech in psychoanalysis. In *Practice and Precept in Psychoanalytic Technique: Selected Papers of R. M. Loewenstein*, pp. 52–67. New Haven, CT: Yale University Press, 1982.

——— (1953). Some remarks on defenses, autonomous ego, and psychoanalytic technique. In *Practice and Precept in Psychoanalytic Technique: Selected Papers of R. M. Loewenstein*, pp. 40–51. New Haven, CT: Yale University Press, 1982.

——— (1962). Some considerations on free association. In *Practice and Precept in Psychoanalytic Technique: Selected Papers of R. M. Loewenstein*, pp. 175–195. New Haven, CT: Yale University Press, 1982.

——— (1966). Defense organization and autonomous ego functions. In *Practice and Precept in Psychoanalytic Technique: Selected Papers of R. M. Loewenstein*, pp. 196–210. New Haven, CT: Yale University Press, 1982.

——— (1971). Ego autonomy and psychoanalytic technique. In

Practice and Precept in Psychoanalytic Technique: Selected Papers of R. M. Loewenstein, pp. 211–228. New Haven, CT: Yale University Press, 1982.

Mahler, M., Pine, F., and Bergman, A. (1975). *The Psychological Birth of the Human Infant*. New York: Basic Books.

Malin, A. (1993). A self-psychological approach to the analysis of resistance: a case report. *International Journal of Psycho-Analysis* 74:505–518.

Mayes, L. C., and Cohen, D. J. (1996). Children's developing theory of mind. *Journal of American Psychoanalytic Association* 44:117–142.

Mitchell, S. A. (1988). *Relational Concepts in Psychoanalysis*. Cambridge, MA: Harvard University Press.

―――― (1993). *Hope and Dread in Psychoanalysis*. New York: Basic Books.

Mitchell, S. A., and Black, M. J. (1995). *Freud and Beyond*. New York: Basic Books.

Novick, J., and Novick, K. K. (1996). *Fearful Symmetry*. Northvale, NJ: Jason Aronson.

Ornstein, A., and Ornstein, P. (1994). On the conceptualization of clinical facts in psychoanalysis. *International Journal of Psycho-Analysis* 75:977–994.

Paniagua, C. (1985). A methodological approach to surface material. *International Review of Psycho-Analysis* 12:311–325.

―――― (1991). Patient's surface, clinical surface, and workable surface. *Journal of the American Psychoanalytic Association* 39:669–685.

Pfeffer, A. (1961). Follow-up study of a satisfactory analysis. *Journal of the American Psychoanalytic Association* 9:698–718.

Piaget, J. (1930). *The Child's Conception of Physical Causality*. London: Kegan Paul.

Piaget, J., and Inhelder, B. (1959). *The Psychology of the Child.* New York: Basic Books.

Pine, F. (1985). *Developmental Theory and Clinical Process.* New Haven, CT: Yale University Press.

———— (1988). Four psychologies of psychoanalysis and their place in clinical work. *Journal of the American Psychoanalytic Association* 36:571–596.

Pray, M. (1994). Analyzing defenses: two different methods. *Journal of Clinical Psychoanalysis* 3:87–126.

Rabin, H. M. (1995). The liberating effect on the analyst of the paradigm shift in psychoanalysis. *Psychoanalytic Psychology* 12:467–482.

Rapaport, D. (1951). The autonomy of the ego. In *The Collected Papers of David Rapaport*, ed. M. M. Gill, pp. 357–367. New York: Basic Books, 1967.

———— (1954). Clinical implications of ego psychology. In *The Collected Papers of David Rapaport*, ed. M. M. Gill, pp. 586–593. New York: Basic Books, 1967.

———— (1956). Present-day ego psychology. In *The Collected Papers of David Rapaport*, ed. M. M. Gill, pp. 594–623. New York: Basic Books, 1967.

———— (1957). The theory of ego autonomy: a generalization. In *The Collected Papers of David Rapaport*, ed. M. M. Gill, pp. 722–744. New York: Basic Books, 1967.

———— (1967). *The Collected Papers of David Rapaport*, ed. M. M. Gill. New York: Basic Books.

Raphling, D. L. (1992). Some vicissitudes of aggression in the interpretive process. *Psychoanalytic Quarterly* 61:352–369.

Reich, W. (1993). *Character Analysis.* New York: Farrar, Straus & Cudahy, 1949.

Renik, O. (1993). Analytic interaction: conceptualizing technique in light of the analyst's irreducible subjectivity. *Psychoanalytic Quarterly* 62:553–571.

——— (1995a). The role of the analyst's expectations in clinical technique: reflections on the concept of resistance. *Journal of the American Psychoanalytic Association* 43:83–94.

——— (1995b). The ideal of the anonymous analyst and the problem of self disclosure. *Psychoanalytic Quarterly* 64:466–495.

——— (1996). The perils of neutrality. *Psychoanalytic Quarterly* 65:495–517.

Richards, A. D. (1986). Introduction. In *The Science of Mental Conflict: Essays in Honor of Charles Brenner*, ed. A. D. Richards and M. S. Willick, pp. 1–28. Hillsdale, NJ: Analytic Press.

——— (1992). Unconscious fantasy: an introduction to the work of Jacob A. Arlow, M. D., and to the symposium in his honor. *Journal of Clinical Psychoanalysis* 1:505–512.

——— (1995). A. A. Brill: the politics of exclusion and the politics of pluralism. Presented at the New York Psychoanalytic Society as the 47th A. A. Brill Lecture, November.

Sachs, O. (1967). Distinction between fantasy and reality elements in memory and reconstruction. *International Journal of Psycho-Analysis* 48:416–423.

Sandler, A. M. (1975). Comments on the significance of Piaget's work for psychoanalysis. *International Review of Psycho-Analysis* 2:365–377.

Sandler, J., Person, E. S., and Fonagy, P. (1991). Introduction. In *Freud's "On Narcissism: An Introduction,"* pp. ix–xx. New Haven: Yale University Press.

Schacter, D. L. (1996). *Searching for Memory*. New York: Basic Books.

Schafer, R. (1983). *The Analytic Attitude*. New York: Basic Books.

———— (1985). The concept of psychic reality, developmental influences, and unconscious communications. *Journal of the American Psychoanalytic Association* 33:537–554.

———— (1994). The contemporary Kleinians of London. *Psychoanalytic Quarterly* 63:409–432.

Schlessinger, N., and Robbins, F. (1983). *A Developmental View of the Psychoanalytic Process: Follow-up Studies and Their Consequences*. New York: International Universities Press.

Searl, M. N. (1936). Some queries on principles of technique. *International Journal of Psycho-Analysis* 17:471–493.

Siegler, R. (1991). *Children's Thinking*. Englewood Cliffs, NJ: Prentice Hall.

Silverman, M. A. (1987). Clinical material. *Psychoanalytic Inquiry* 7:147–166.

Singer, E. (1977). The function of analytic anonymity. In *The Human Dimension in Psychoanalysis*, ed. K. A. Frank, pp. 181–192. New York: Grune & Stratton.

Spezzano, C. (1993). *Affect in Psychoanalysis*. Hillsdale, NJ: Analytic Press.

Spitz, R. A. (1945). Hospitalism: an inquiry into the genesis of psychiatric conditions in early childhood. *Psychoanalytic Study of the Child* 1:53–74. New York: International Universities Press.

———— (1946). Hospitalism: a follow up report. *Psychoanalytic Study of the Child* 2:113–117. New York: International Universities Press.

Sterba, R. (1934). The fate of the ego in psychoanalytic therapy. *International Journal of Psycho-Analysis* 15:117–126.

Strachey, J. (1934). The nature of the therapeutic action of psychoanalysis. *International Journal of Psycho-Analysis* 15:127–159.

212 References

Thompson, M. G. (1985). *The Death of Desire*. New York: New York University Press.

Wallerstein, R. (1988). One psychoanalysis or many? *International Journal of Psycho-Analysis* 69:5–22.

Winnicott, D. W. (1960). The theory of the patient–infant relationship. In *The Maturational Processes and the Facilitating Environment*, pp. 37–55. New York: International Universities Press, 1965.

——— (1986). *Holding and Interpretation*. London: Hogarth.

Wolf, E. S. (1988). *Treating the Self*. New York: Guilford.

Yorke, C. (1991). Freud's "On Narcissism": A Teaching Text. In *Freud's "On Narcissism: An Introduction,"* ed. J. Sandler, E. S. Person, and P. Fonagy, pp. 35–53. New Haven: Yale University Press.

Zetzel, E. (1968). The so-called good hysteric. *International Journal of Psycho-Analysis* 49:256–260.

Index